THE ADMINISTRATION OF THE CHURCH AND THE MINISTRY OF THE WORD

Witness Lee

Living Stream Ministry
Anaheim, CA • www.lsm.org

© 2007 Living Stream Ministry

All rights reserved. No part of this work may be reproduced or transmitted in any form or by any means—graphic, electronic, or mechanical, including photocopying, recording, or information storage and retrieval systems—without written permission from the publisher.

First Edition, April 2007.

ISBN 0-7363-3243-X

Published by

Living Stream Ministry
2431 W. La Palma Ave., Anaheim, CA 92801 U.S.A.
P. O. Box 2121, Anaheim, CA 92814 U.S.A.

Printed in the United States of America

07 08 09 10 11 12 / 9 8 7 6 5 4 3 2

CONTENTS

Title	Page
Preface	5
1 The Building Up of the Church	7
2 Problems in the Administration of the Church and the Ministry of the Word	17
3 Not Doing a Tearing Down Work in the Church Service	33
4 The Significance of Building Revealed in John 14	43
5 The Oneness in John 17	55
6 Building Up in Love and Knowing People	71
7 The Building of the Church Requiring an Absolute Consecration	85
8 The Building Up of the Church Requiring Knowledge of Different Matters	95
9 The Meaning of Building Being in the Building of God's Authority over Man	105
10 Selecting Material for the Ministry of the Word	119
11 The Importance and the Commission of the Ministry of the Word	133
12 The Word Being to Supply and Administration Being for Building Up	149
13 The Ground for the Building of the Church	167
14 The Recovery of the Church Ground	175

PREFACE

This book is composed of messages given by Brother Witness Lee in service meetings held in Taipei in September 1957. It contains fourteen chapters concerning the importance of the administration of the church and the ministry of the word and the problems arising in them, the building of the church, and the practice of the recovery of the ground of the church. These messages have been translated from the original Chinese.

Chapter One

THE BUILDING UP OF THE CHURCH

Scripture Reading: Matt. 16:18; Eph. 4:11, 16; 2:20; 1 Pet. 2:5; 1 Cor. 3:9-10, 14; 14:4-5, 12, 26; Heb. 11:10

GOD'S INTENTION BEING TO RECOVER THE BUILDING UP OF THE CHURCH

In this chapter we will fellowship concerning the building up of the church. Over the past two thousand years people have not paid sufficient attention to the matter of building. Over the last few centuries God has recovered many items. These items of recovery have occupied God's children so much that they have not had the energy to see God's further recovery. Strictly speaking, there has not been much recovery concerning the matter of building. Only in recent years has God led His people to consider this matter.

It has been difficult for us to find topics related to building up in Christian publications. Many people speak of edification, but few speak of building up. Therefore, in the English translations of the Bible, the Greek word for building up is often translated as "edification" instead of "building up." This is also the case with the Chinese translation of the Bible. Many portions that are translated as "edification" should actually be "building up."

THE SAINTS BEING BUILT UP AS A SPIRITUAL HOUSE

In Greek the verb for *building up* has the same root as the noun *house*. If the word for *build up* is translated as "edify," it conveys only the thought of education rather than the meaning of building. We need to see the difference between *building up* and *edification*. In the past we had a regard for edification but not for building up. We understood edification as a matter of individual experience and had no consciousness of its relation to corporate building up. However, in the Bible building refers not only to individuals being edified but also to the saints being built together. In other words, according to the Scriptures, building includes not only personal edification but also the saints being built up as a spiritual house (1 Pet. 2:5). Edification is needed for individual matters, and building up is needed for corporate matters.

BUILDING UP THE BODY OF CHRIST

Since the words for *building up* and *house* have the same root in Greek, *building up* means to build all the saints up as a house. In spiritual terms it is to build them up as the Body (Eph. 2:20-22; 4:12). Our physical body can be compared to a house. Second Corinthians 5:1 refers to our body as a tabernacle, because our body is temporal. This verse also indicates that the transfigured body we will have in the future is a building from God, an eternal dwelling in the heavens.

The church is the house of God (Eph. 2:22) and the Body of Christ (4:12). Although the house of God and the Body of Christ indicate two aspects of the church, they refer to the same thing, because the Body of Christ is a spiritual house. First Corinthians 6:19 says that our body is a temple of the Holy Spirit. Our body is a temple, a building. When the Lord Jesus said, "Destroy this temple, and in three days I will raise it up" (John 2:19), He was saying that if the Jews destroyed His body and killed Him, He would raise it up in three days. This shows that in the Bible, the body refers to a house, and the house refers to the temple. The church is the house of God and the Body of Christ; these are two aspects of one thing.

If the church is merely the Body, we may think that there is no need for building up; however, the Body is also a house. Hence, there is the need for building up. The Bible speaks of building a spiritual house (1 Pet. 2:5), the building of a dwelling place of God in spirit (Eph. 2:22), and also the building up of the Body of Christ (4:12). If we cannot apprehend the fact that the Body is a house, we will question the need for the Body to be built up.

THE BUILDING IN THE NEW TESTAMENT

May the Lord grant those of us who serve together a deep feeling that He needs a strong recovery. He needs a recovery of the building up. Building goes beyond edification. Our work is not merely for the edification of the saints in general; rather, it is to build up a Body, a spiritual house. Ephesians 4:11-12 says, "He Himself gave some as apostles and some as prophets and some as evangelists and some as shepherds and teachers, for the perfecting of the saints unto the work of the ministry, unto the building up of the Body of Christ." The gifted ones are for the building up of the Body of Christ.

In Matthew 16:18 the Lord said, "I will build My church." Ephesians 2:22 says that in Christ the Jews and Gentiles are "being built together into a dwelling place of God in spirit." First Peter 2:5 says that we, "as living stones, are being built up as a spiritual house." First Corinthians 3:10 says that Paul, as a wise master builder, laid a foundation and that we should take heed how we build upon it. We should build with gold, silver, and precious stones (v. 12). Chapter 14 emphasizes earnestly desiring spiritual gifts for the sake of building up (vv. 1, 3-5, 12). This means that all the gifts should be for the building up of the church.

According to the verses above, God's desire in this age is to build the church, which is His house, the Body of Christ. Man dwells in his body and also in a house. Both are a dwelling place for man. When a person departs from the world, he is unclothed from his body. This means that he leaves his body, his dwelling place on earth. God's work in this age is to build a dwelling place for Himself.

THE BUILDING UP OF THE CHURCH BEING THE BUILDING UP OF THE NEW JERUSALEM

Hebrews 11:10 says that Abraham "eagerly waited for the city which has the foundations, whose Architect and Builder is God." The city with the foundations is the coming New Jerusalem. The New Jerusalem is the tabernacle of God with men (Rev. 21:3). In other words, the New Jerusalem is God's dwelling place. This does not mean that God has two different buildings in this age. He does not have the church on earth as one building and the holy city, the New Jerusalem, in the heavens as another city. God is not temporarily dwelling in the church today only to discard the church and move to the New Jerusalem in the future. The church and the New Jerusalem are one.

When God builds up the church, He is building up the New Jerusalem. These are two aspects of the same work. The church is the temple of God, the house of God, but in the New Jerusalem we will not see a temple (v. 22), because the temple will be enlarged into a city. The building of the temple is not one work, and the building of the city, another work. The coming New Jerusalem is the consummation of the church. The temple is enlarged to be a city.

In this age God's only work is building. Although His building work is on earth, it is heavenly. Although His building work is in time, it is eternal. Although God is building up the church on earth, this building is in the heavenly realm. Although God is building up the church in time, this building is eternal. The New Jerusalem is heavenly; it is full of the heavenly nature and the heavenly flavor.

The ultimate goal of God's work in this age is the building of a dwelling place for Himself. In its initial stage it is a house, and in its mature stage it will be a city, which is the tabernacle of God with men. In the Old Testament the tabernacle of God is the temple of God. In the New Testament the church is the tabernacle of God and the temple of God. The New Jerusalem will be the tabernacle of God with men. There will be no temple in the New Jerusalem because everything will have reached maturity. The city is a tabernacle as well as an enlarged temple.

THE CENTRAL WORK OF GOD BEING THE BUILDING

The central work of God is the building. The building is not a matter of understanding doctrines, saving sinners, or even edifying the saints. Even though the New Testament refers to the edification of individual saints, its focus is on the building of God's house. We often have strong feelings concerning saving sinners and edifying the saints, but we lack feeling concerning building God's house. This does not mean that we should not pay attention to saving sinners and edifying the saints, but we need to see the ultimate goal of God's work in this age.

Since Paul had a clear vision concerning the building, he said, "As a wise master builder I have laid a foundation, and another builds upon it. But let each man take heed how he builds upon it" (1 Cor. 3:10). We need to be careful concerning the way we build, the materials we build with, and the outcome of our building. May the brothers and sisters see that saving sinners and edifying the saints are related to the central goal of building God's house. If we pay attention to this central work, our preaching the gospel to save sinners will be more effective, and our edification of the saints will not cause problems. For example, our shortage in building God's house is the basic reason the brothers and sisters in Taipei do not seem to have the strength to preach the gospel. The key is the building of God's house. If God's house, the Body of Christ, can be built up, saving sinners and edifying the saints will be very easy.

THE KEY TO THE BUILDING UP OF THE CHURCH—
THE ADMINISTRATION OF THE CHURCH AND
THE MINISTRY OF THE WORD

The two most important matters in the building up of the church, God's house, are the administration of the church and the ministry of the word. If the administration of a local church is poor, there will not be much building in that church. Similarly, if the ministry of the word is poor in a local church, there will not be much building there. We have used the word *edification* for so many years, but we now need to use the word *building*. The individual saints need to be edified, but the church as a corporate entity, as the Body of Christ and the house of God, needs to be built up. The building up of the church depends on the administration of the church and the ministry of the word.

According to the New Testament, all our speaking should be for the building up of the church. In 1 Corinthians 14:12 Paul says, "Since you are zealous of spirits, seek that you may excel for the building up of the church." Verse 1 says, "Pursue love, and desire earnestly spiritual gifts, but especially that you may prophesy." The gift that excels in building up the church is prophesying, because prophesying is a matter of the ministry of the word. In 1 and 2 Timothy, when the church was in a desolate situation, there was the need for the administration of the church in addition to the ministry of the word. The responsibility for the administration of the church is with the elders. After the church became desolate, the apostle spoke of the administration of the church in the books of 1 and 2 Timothy and Titus. The administration of the church becomes crucial when the church is in desolation and confusion.

The administration of the church and other matters related to the elders are not spoken of in the book of Romans. However, the books of 1 and 2 Timothy and Titus clearly speak of the administration by the elders, because the church had become desolate at that time. If we know the principle of the Bible, we will understand the meaning of the Holy Spirit. In the initial stage of the church God led and built up the church by the ministry of the word. However, at a certain time the ministry of the word was not sufficient; there was the need for the administration of the church. Hence, in the books of 1 and 2 Timothy we see both the administration of the church and the ministry of the word. Paul says, "The things which you have heard from me through many witnesses, these commit to faithful men, who will be competent to teach others also" (2 Tim. 2:2). Here we see the ministry of the word and the administration of the church.

After the church had been established for a period of time, there was the need for the administration of the church as well as the ministry of the word. Both are necessary for the building up of the church. If the administration of a local church and the ministry of the word are poor, the church will not be built up. When the administration of the church and the ministry of the word are strong, the church can be built up. May the Lord open our eyes to see that the central work of God in this age is His building; He wants to build His house, the Body of Christ, the church. Since we have a part in this building, we must see the administration of the church and the ministry of the word. The ministry of the word is related to gift, and the administration of the church is related to office. Both of these aspects are for the building up of the church. Our speaking as prophets is for the ministry of the word and is related to the aspect of gift. The serving of the elders is for the administration of the church and is related to the aspect of office.

LEARNING THE PRINCIPLES FOR ADMINISTRATING THE CHURCH AND MINISTERING THE WORD

We might not all be able to speak and fulfill the ministry of the word as prophets, nor can all of us administrate the church as elders. Nevertheless, there should be good elders and those who can minister the word in a strong way among us. In principle, those who have a part in God's work should learn to administrate the church and minister the word. Although the sisters, standing in the position of having their heads covered, should not be elders, in principle they should learn to administrate as elders. Everyone who has a part in God's building work should learn to administrate the church and minister the word. Every serving one should know the administration of the church and the ministry of the word. If we do not know these two matters, we are unskilled in God's work. The administration of the church and the ministry of the word are two lessons that we must learn, because the building up of the church depends on both.

The progress of the church first requires the administration of the church and then the ministry of the word. The sequence in the Bible, however, first presents the ministry of the word and then the administration of the church. When the condition of the church is normal, the administration of the church is not as crucial. But when the church becomes desolate and disorderly, there is a need for the administration of the church and the ministry of the word. The ministry of the word and the administration of the church go together; it is difficult to say which is first and which is second. Therefore, the brothers, especially those who minister the word and those who serve as elders, need to see the responsibility they bear. The condition of God's building, that is, whether a local church is strong or weak, depends on the administration carried out by the elders and the word released by the ministry. The elders and those who minister the word are skilled workers. They are assisted by others who are not as skilled. This can be compared to building a house with workers who are skilled and with others who are not as skilled. Whenever the skilled workers are weak, the administration of the church and the ministry of the word are weak in that church, and the workers who are not as skilled will be confused and not know what to do. But whenever the skilled workers are strong in carrying out the work, it is easy for other workers to cooperate.

This is the condition of the local church. When the ministry of the word and the administration of the church are strong, the brothers and sisters who are not as skilled can have a beautiful coordination. However, when the administration by the elders and the ministry of the word are weak, the church will be in disorder even if the brothers and sisters are busy zealously preaching the gospel and edifying the saints. In such a situation the building will not be accomplished, because the more they "build," the more they tear down. The building up of the church depends on the administration of the church and the ministry of the word. Those who are involved with the work must know the principle of the administration of the church and the ministry of the word.

THE CONDITION OF THE ADMINISTRATION OF THE CHURCH AND THE MINISTRY OF THE WORD DEPENDING ON OUR PERSON

The condition of the administration of the church and the ministry of the word depends on our person. Our person determines the condition of the administration of the church and the ministry of the word. The central work of God is His building, which depends on the administration of the church and the ministry of the word. The kind of person we are determines how we administer the church and minister the word. The administration of the church and the ministry of the word cannot be separated from our person. This is similar to the fact that houses built by Westerners have a Western appearance, and those built by Chinese have a Chinese appearance. We build according to our person. This is especially true in spiritual matters. For this reason it is inadequate merely to study how to administrate the church and minister the word. Rather, we must see that the way is our person. The way to administrate the church is related to the person who administrates. The kind of person we are determines how we administrate. It is inadequate for us to merely learn an outward way; we must deal with our person.

After a long period of unrest, God gave me the feeling within that He is doing a building work in this age. In Manila I released over fifteen messages related to the building. When I went to Hong Kong, the brothers wanted me to perfect them in certain matters. I pointed out to the serving ones that it is inadequate simply to be busy. We must see that God desires a building. During this period of time in Taipei, I have much feeling concerning God's building and the serving ones. When I view these two together, I have deep sorrow and a burden within because our condition is far from God's building.

GOD'S BUILDING BEING ACCOMPLISHED
WHEN OUR PERSON IS DEALT WITH

God wants to take the way of building, but the problem He encounters is our person. We are the problem. Those who administrate the church and minister the word are full of problems. Our way and our doctrine are not the problem; rather, our poor condition is the problem. We have come to a critical juncture in our service. The church in Taipei has been here for eight years, from 1949 to 1957. If we continue as we are, our work will have no result. We will only have endless problems and continual loss; there will be no increase in blessing. As long as the serving ones continue according to the traditional way, our work will have no future. For the sake of God's building and the future of the work, may the Lord have mercy on us so that we would see that the problem is not with our doctrine or practice but with our person.

We need to consider the condition of our work and our present situation before the Lord. This does not mean that we should be introspective. We need to receive light and be helped by this fellowship. We need to be calm before the Lord and allow Him to shine on us, speak to us, touch us, and deal with us. Unless we have passed through the Lord's dealing hand, much of our outward activity is vain and meaningless.

If God does not deal with us thoroughly, His building will not be accomplished, regardless of the methods we use. For God's building to be accomplished in a proper way, He needs to deal with us strongly in the matters of the administration of the church and the ministry of the word. In the administration of the church the brothers who serve as elders need to be dealt with. Those who speak for God also need to be dealt with. Otherwise, our administration of the church and our speaking will not result in the reality of building. May we all have a heart that fears the Lord to see that the building up of the church depends on the person of those who administrate the church and those who minister the word. If we allow God to deal with us, our work will have impact even if our method is inferior. Otherwise, our work will tear down the building regardless of the method we use.

Today God is concerned with the building. The building depends on the condition of our person. May we all be calm before the Lord and allow Him to shine on us and speak to us.

CHAPTER TWO

PROBLEMS IN THE ADMINISTRATION OF THE CHURCH AND THE MINISTRY OF THE WORD

THE FIRST PROBLEM—NOT HAVING A BURDEN

The greatest problem in the administration of the church and the ministry of the word is not having a burden or, we can say, not receiving a burden or not paying attention to a burden. It is possible for elders to administrate the church without a burden. Those who minister the word may also do so without a burden. The discharge of our burden when we minister the word does not depend on how well we speak. If our only desire is to speak well in order to touch people, our speaking will be without a burden. Likewise, an ability to administrate the church does not discharge one's burden. It is not a matter of how well we can administrate but whether our administration is effective and can touch people.

For example, when people come to a meeting, there may be the need to release the word. We must seek the Lord concerning what we speak and concerning the issue of our speaking. It is not a matter of how well we speak, the logistics of our presentation, or whether the saints are touched; rather, it is a matter of what will be produced in the saints. If some are not yet saved, we should receive a burden to bear their souls by the Lord's grace to sow the seed of salvation into them when we release the word. Our burden is salvation, not the release of a dynamic word. If they are saved but do not love the Lord, our burden should be for them to love the Lord. If they love the Lord but are not willing to give themselves to the Lord and receive His dealing, our burden should be for them to willingly give themselves to the Lord and be dealt with by Him. This is the ministry of the word with a burden.

Otherwise, our Lord's Day message meeting may easily fall into the condition of the so-called Sunday service. Every week someone is assigned to release a message in order to maintain the meeting. After the meeting, everyone goes home, eats lunch, rests, and returns in the evening for the bread-breaking meeting. This is a Sunday service. In this situation those who minister the word must receive a burden. We need to know the condition of those who come to listen to a message. They might not have any feeling concerning their own condition, but we need to be clear and full of feeling concerning their condition. They may be able to sit and listen peacefully week after week, but we cannot speak peacefully week after week. We need to receive the burden to "disturb" and "trouble" them so that even if they come to the meeting peacefully, they will be inwardly disturbed when they leave.

If we are not concerned that our speaking does not produce any effect in those who listen, we do not have a burden. This situation indicates that those who speak and those who listen are in a routine. This is the condition of degraded Christianity where the congregation routinely listens to the pastor, and the pastor routinely preaches to the congregation year after year. This should not be our practice. The ministry of the word should enlighten those who hear. When we minister the word every Lord's Day, we should "trouble" people to the extent that they have no peace. This is what it means to have a burden.

If the listeners are lukewarm, even though they may listen peacefully, those who minister the word should not be at peace. They should go before the Lord, and let Him take away their peace, even to the point of losing sleep and not eating until they receive a burden from the Lord. Then their speaking will enable the Holy Spirit to work in the listeners. Only this kind of speaking is the speaking of God. Brothers who minister the word must have a burden, not merely doctrines, logic, and examples. Ministering the word in this way is intolerable; it is an offense to God, and it is a sin in His eyes.

Receiving the Burden to Speak God's Word in the Ministry of the Word

In Isaiah 13:1 the Chinese Union Version says that the prophets received inspiration when they spoke for God. The Hebrew word for *inspiration,* however, means "burden." Man needs to receive a burden. We cannot neglect this responsibility and think that God has not given us a burden. The Epistles of Paul clearly show that he received burdens. When someone in the church in Corinth committed the sin of fornication, Paul did not simply condemn the sin or stop praying for the one who sinned. He received a burden from God to bear a responsibility and commission for the church (1 Cor. 5:1-13). Paul did not preach doctrines in his Epistles; instead, he was burdened to fellowship concerning certain matters, so he was able to touch people's feeling.

There is a danger that the ministry of the word in the church in Taipei may become the same as the preaching of sermons in Sunday services. When we minister the word of God, our concern should be whether we have God's speaking, not the topic of our speaking. In order to have God's speaking, the one who ministers the word must have a burden. People may have a negative reaction or be stirred up when they hear a message that is spoken with a burden, but they cannot deny that it is God's speaking. This kind of message can help people and solve their problems. A message that sounds nice but is void of God's speaking cannot touch people, turn them inwardly, or satisfy those who are hungry and thirsty, because they are not the words that God wants to speak even if they are from the Bible.

Therefore, speaking should not be easy or cheap. We cannot speak simply because we have prepared a message. One who ministers the word should bear people's condition before God. He bears the responsibility of knowing their needs. He needs to sense their condition and know what God wants to speak. The help we have received from training cannot replace the burden that is within us. The danger is that the burden has been replaced so that we are short of revelation and spiritual burden.

Being Desperate for People's Situation to Preach the Effective Word

Fifty-two weeks a year there is a message meeting in the church in Taipei on the Lord's Day. Do the brothers who minister the word fast and pray before ministering the word? Of course, there is no regulation that requires the brothers to fast and pray, as this would be useless. The brothers need to understand that bearing the word of God is equal to bearing the souls of man. The saints come to the meetings week after week to listen to our speaking, so we must bear them. If there is no change in them after three months, we should not be at peace. This can be compared to a merchant who is unable to sleep peacefully when he has no business for two weeks and who is unable to eat when there is no profit after three months. He will be full of sorrow and concern.

Many brothers and sisters with businesses come to me. Although they simply sit without opening their mouths, I can sense the heavy burden within them and realize that they have encountered difficulties in their business. Are the brothers who speak sorrowful for the souls who have not changed in three months? A store owner who has no customers would be unable to continue working, considering everything to be fine. He would consider the situation and find a way to change the situation. How can those who minister the word continue as usual when there is no profit? We should not consider that it is sufficient merely to speak from the podium week after week.

When Brother Nee began his work in Foochow, he fasted and prayed every Saturday for the gospel meeting on the Lord's Day. He considered before the Lord what to speak and how to speak. He considered what word the sinners needed to hear. Since he fasted and prayed with a heavy burden, his words were always very effective and were later published as messages. Many who are used by the Lord bear a burden in their ministry of the word. When Peace Wang was young, she had a successful revival work. She always knelt before the Lord and spent a long period of time weeping and grieving for sinners. Therefore, when she stood up to speak, her words were always living and operative.

Serving with a Burden

We have a good order in our service, but we are lacking in burden. Having a burden means that we have a goal which we must reach. If we have not reached our goal or are unable to produce the expected result, we should be concerned. If we are able to serve, even though there is no result, we do not have a burden. This attitude indicates a lack of burden. Our speaking should never fall into this. Hence, the brothers who minister the word must bear a heavy burden before the Lord, having no peace to rest or eat and even troubling others so that they also have no peace. This can be compared to the city of Jerusalem having no peace when the Lord Jesus was born (Matt. 2:1-18). Those who speak for the Lord must have a feeling to trouble the saints to the point that they have no peace inwardly. When they have no peace, we can have peace. The saints cannot love the world and love the Lord. They must not be lukewarm. Those who serve the Lord need to have this kind of burden.

Many serve as employees in a big company. They work a fixed number of hours every day and simply do the tasks that are assigned to them. They do not make big mistakes and are not concerned whether the company makes a profit. They are employees without a burden; they serve without a burden. If we make no profit on the first day of our business, we should be concerned about our livelihood. If the serving brothers, whether they serve in the children's work or the young people's work, have this kind of consciousness, they will succeed. Complaining that we fail because we are weak shows that we lack a burden. Every serving one must be burdened to the extent that he feels responsible if the work does not succeed. He should be like a businessman who thinks of his business even in his sleep.

Discerning between the Service of Responsibility and the Service of Burden

The elders in all the churches must come before the Lord to receive a burden and to see if all the home meetings in their localities are satisfactory. We must have a concern for the condition of the meetings. Are they strong or weak, living or dead, rich or poor? We cannot remain unchanged. Perhaps those responsible for the home meetings are at peace, but the elders should not be at peace. The elders should coordinate together and not act individualistically. They should bear a corporate burden to completely change the condition of the home meetings. They need to pray for the saints, even with tears, and seek the Lord for the proper words to speak to them. Then they should speak in the meetings according to their burden until the saints become uneasy within and are not content with their present situation.

Such a speaking by the elders is not according to arrangement but according to burden. The elders should have a burden; they should not merely bear responsibility. As elders, we should not simply fellowship and discuss the condition of the different home meetings, visit them, and give an evaluation report at the next elders' meeting. There is no burden in such a practice; it will be ineffective and not result in any profit. If we have a company with many employees, its yearly earnings will not be influenced by discussions, reports, and evaluations. These do not carry out the burden. If we have a real burden, we will set a goal for our yearly profit, work toward this goal, and be determined to reach it.

Both in the administration of the church and in the ministry of the word, the brothers are commendable in their bearing of responsibility. However, they lack a burden. Without a burden, all our activity will be dead and ineffective; with a burden, we will be living and flourishing. Such an outcome is not related to our method but to our person.

Serving with a Burden
Causing the Self to Be Dealt With

Children will never be successful in their studies if they study only for their tests. If they have a burden, their studying will change. A brother may give a message merely out of obligation, because it is his turn to speak. However, giving messages is not a matter of obligation but of burden. We may speak for half a year, but those who listen might not receive anything, and our speaking will be in vain. If we have a burden, we will see that our messages are ineffective. Our messages should "trouble" people so that they have no peace and stir them up to love and serve the Lord. In this situation, our being will be touched by God. There is no need for the self to be dealt with if we give messages that are out of obligation. However, in giving a message out of a burden, our self must be dealt with.

Working from nine to six as an employee is a matter of obligation and does not require any dealing. However, we would work differently if we had our own business. Our laziness would be dealt with because we would rise earlier to work. The attitude of a waiter or clerk toward customers might not need to be dealt with. However, a person who owns his shop will adjust himself in order not to offend his customers. Instead of being dealt with, some brothers seem to have more problems because they serve out of obligation, not burden. If there is a burden, our self decreases and is dealt with. It will not increase, because there are things that our burden will not allow us to do, and there are areas that will require our being dealt with before we can release our burden. Hence, having a burden deals with us the most.

A young man who is not burdened with a family can be carefree in his living. However, after he is married and has children, he will know the meaning of being diligent and disciplined. A child can spend his parents' money freely without self-control. But when he is older and lives on his own, his spending is budgeted. He will be more careful when he goes shopping. Spending his parents' money was one thing, but spending his own money is a burden. It seems as if the brothers in the churches serve according to obligation as employees in a company. They do not seem to have much burden. Such service is dangerous and will cause us to lose the Lord's presence.

Everyone Receiving a Burden
and Serving the Lord according to Burden

Everyone who serves the Lord must receive a burden and have a burden. This also applies to the sisters even though they are not involved in the church administration or in giving messages. If the sisters fellowship together and visit people simply because it is time to do so, they are doing so out of obligation. The sisters should seek to know the result of their fellowship and visitation. They should know the condition of the sisters under their care. They should not say, "As long as the Lord works in them, they will be all right, but if the Lord does not work in them, there is nothing we can do." We must receive a genuine burden.

Even though many sisters have the desire to serve the Lord, few have risen up to serve the Lord lately. The brothers, however, continue to serve as usual. We should sense that the situation with the sisters is not right and receive the burden to stir them up. We also need to study the result of our gospel preaching. We should consider why many remain unsaved even though there are so many sinners. Some brothers should rise up to receive the burden to preach the gospel until someone is saved. We must have a burden.

The problem is that we are gradually leaning toward responsibility in our service; we lack a burden. Since our prayers are mostly without burden, our prayer meetings are ineffective. If someone is saved when we preach the gospel, we thank and praise the Lord. If no one is saved, we are at peace. When we give messages, we are at peace even if there is no effect. The same applies to the administration of the church and visiting the brothers and sisters; we are at peace even if there is no result. Since this is our condition, our prayer is a prayer of obligation, not a prayer with burden. If we pray with a burden, our prayer meeting will be different. Some brothers and sisters will weep bitterly and mourn in prayer, feeling that they cannot go on in the same way. They will feel that the gospel preaching, the administration of the church, and the condition of their meeting are unsatisfactory. This kind of prayer is out of a burden.

Some say that it is easy to lose their burden after a period of time. However, those who have been shown mercy receive burdens continually. It is a serious problem if our burden disappears after we have worked for some time. However, a Christian can continue to work out of obligation even though he has no burden, because his conscience will bother him if he stops working. Whenever our service becomes a matter of fulfilling an obligation, our service has already degraded.

PROBLEMS IN THE ADMINISTRATION OF THE CHURCH

Genuine service is not a matter of obligation but a matter of burden; burden always goes beyond obligation.

THE SECOND PROBLEM—
LACKING A FEELING FOR COORDINATION

Another problem among us is that although the serving ones are capable, they do not have a feeling for coordination in their spirit when they come together to serve. It seems as if everyone is able to serve without others. Consequently, few among us have the spirit of a learner and the spirit of needing help. Those who truly coordinate in spirit should have a strong feeling that they cannot do anything without the help and coordination of others. Our present coordination is one of formality. They do their part without needing anyone else. We may not argue, but there is not much interdependence in spirit. This shows that our spirit of service is improper.

This is the situation of those who work with the young people and the children. The coordination is formal; everyone does what he should do when it is his turn. This is cooperation, not coordination. Coordination means that we cannot do anything without one another. There is a sense that we need others and that others need us. Those who work with young people should be like this; all the service of the church should also be like this. It is normal when the deacons and elders mutually need one another, and the saints feel that they cannot do anything without the elders and deacons.

Today we have rules and arrangements. The elders do things pertaining to elders, and the deacons do things pertaining to deacons. Everyone works when it is his turn. However, we do not have a deep feeling that we cannot go on without the elders and deacons in our service. Some brothers not only lack a sense of the need for the elders and deacons, but they even think that elders and deacons are unnecessary. This is dangerous.

Having the Greatest Form of Pride

Those who live in the workers' home are bright and capable. They seem to be independent and do not need others. This is very dangerous because it is the greatest form of pride. If four brothers are living in the workers' home, they should depend on one another, and others should sense their dependence on one another. Sadly, this is not the atmosphere among us. For example, if it is my turn to preach the gospel, I will either do everything or do nothing. From the human perspective, this may be considered to be coordination, but this coordination is according to regulation and arrangement. There is no sense of needing others in spirit. Some may think that coordination is unnecessary and troublesome and that it is better to not coordinate.

Those who do not need to coordinate are dry, lack blessing, and useless. The fact that we are clever, capable, and do not need one another's help is a great danger. This is a sad and pitiful situation. The fearful thing is that this situation is hidden and not very apparent. This situation can be compared to leprosy. If it is manifested, it is easier to deal with it.

This shows that we lack the fellowship of the Body. When we come together, we seldom have thorough fellowship. For example, when saints from other cities visit Taipei, we sit together for a meeting. After the meeting, however, we all go our separate ways without fellowshipping. This was not our situation during our first six years in Taiwan. In those years, whenever we had a conference, we came together and had much fellowship. Now we are all capable, brilliant, and knowledgeable. We do not need one another; we do not need to fellowship. This is the greatest form of pride. It is the most offensive thing to the Lord and to the Body. We should humbly minister to others and restrict our cleverness through coordination.

Needing Fellowship and Coordination in the Body and in Life

If we lose the principle of coordination and dependence in the Body, we will not be strong in our administration of the church and ministry of the word. Once we lose this principle, we will not have much blessing. Our coordination should not become mechanical, and we should not work only when it is our turn. We should have the feeling that we cannot do anything without others, that we truly need one another. If we come together and assign work, with each doing only his own work, our situation is similar to the division of labor in a civic organization or a large institution. This lack of the flavor of coordination among the members of the Body must be dealt with.

What does it mean to see the Body? The greatest indication that we see the Body is that we cannot be independent. We feel that we need the Body, that we need the brothers and sisters. Presently, however, our coordination can be compared to work in an organization. It seems that we are moving like a machine and that we lack the sense of the fellowship of life.

The Lack of Coordination Producing Criticism

If we lack coordination with others, we will always criticize what they do. Even if we do not express it, we are filled with criticism, and we disapprove of what others do. Such people are narrow and pitiful. In our service we should not expect others to be like us, nor should we expect to be like others. However, because we lack coordination in our service and do not rely and mutually depend on one another, we often step on others. We either do not walk, or we step on others when we do walk. We either do not work, or we do the job of others. We either are not concerned, or we criticize the work of others. When a certain matter is in other's hands, we are not able to do anything, but when an opportunity comes to us, we do it according to our way and discard the help of others. Although this condition is not apparent among us, it will be in our future, because we are not willing to submit to others. This is a foolish way.

Not Requiring Others to Be the Same as We, but Respecting What Others Do

We should not require others to be the same as we are in everything. We should not discuss the way others give messages, visit people, or live. Even if we are not pleased with the way others live, we cannot set standards for others, nor are we qualified to judge others. Only the Lord is the criterion and the Judge. We need to learn to respect what others do. When we speak of being zealous, we should respect others' quietness; when we speak of being calm and joined to the Lord, we should not criticize those who are busy. If everyone is the same as we are, there will not be the Body. There would be only one member. This is not the church. If everyone is like us, there would be only we ourselves and not the church. The church is composed of many kinds of people. This can be compared to the human body having different members. The hands look like hands, the feet look like feet, the ears look like ears, and the eyes look like eyes. Even the member who seems to be the most uncomely is necessary in the Body.

Hence, we should learn not to step on others. When it is our turn to work, we should not criticize what others have done. It is a blessing to respect the work of others and to add our work to theirs. We should be positive when we speak with others, not negative. It is unwise to say that others are wrong. As long as these negative factors exist among us, the administration of the church will have problems, and the ministry of the word will not be strong. Many saints from different places serve together in the church. They have different dispositions and family backgrounds, and they also have different spiritual backgrounds and training. Therefore, we cannot expect everyone to be like we are. We need to learn not to step on others. When we take a step, we should not step on others. We should especially avoid stepping on others when we minister the word.

For example, when speaking about prayer, we should not criticize those who speak about meditation, because the saints may need both. We should simply speak positively about prayer without criticizing others' speaking concerning meditation. When we serve together, we must absolutely avoid criticizing others in the ministry of the word. Some may speak about prayer and others about meditating; some may speak of being zealous and others of being in the Holy of Holies. These are not heretical teachings; they are merely different in emphasis. Criticizing others shows that we are narrow, and this will lead to division. If this is the way we work, there will be no building among us; on the contrary, there will be destruction.

We should simply labor positively and learn to receive help from others. We should realize that no one can do our part.

Even the apostle Paul could not do what we can do. However, we also need to admit that we cannot replace others. Every person has his own function. When we minister the word, fellowship, and pray, we should not criticize others. In particular, when we pray with others, we should avoid praying in a contradictory manner.

Not Insisting on Our Own Way

The elders once felt that a certain meeting should study the Gospel of John. One of the responsible brothers in that meeting, however, felt that John was too long and wanted to study 1 Thessalonians instead. He felt this would help those who did not normally read the Bible. Since he insisted, the elders eventually agreed with him even though his burden for 1 Thessalonians was not proper. This brother did not have a proper burden. He simply thought that the saints would be afraid of a book with twenty-one chapters, and he allowed his opinion to trample the feeling of the other brothers. Unless this brother was truly burdened for 1 Thessalonians, he should not have presented it in the service. We should not do things that we have no burden for, and we should not abandon things for which we are burdened; we must serve according to burden. To do otherwise violates a spiritual principle. This responsible brother had not learned the lesson in spiritual matters, and he was inexperienced in the way he conducted himself. If our fellowship is a matter of spiritual burden, there should be no problem with proposing a change, and we should not criticize the burden. However, if we simply want to change others' ways, we should not do this.

We need to respect the ways of the ones with whom we serve. Even though the elders will not force a group to study a certain book or speak certain things, we should not casually change what they commit to us. Strictly speaking, it is all right to study either John or 1 Thessalonians; it does not matter which book is studied. It is possible to minister to the brothers and sisters through 1 Thessalonians and through the Gospel of John. In our service we should always avoid changing the ways of others.

We should realize that when we change others' ways, they might not accept it, because they feel that it is inappropriate, and if they accept our change, there is not a sweet feeling. Because of this kind of problem, our service in the administration of the church and the ministry of the word is not strong. Even in the world, when people work together, it is not easy to change one another's ways. If we truly have a skill, it will be manifested if we work according to their way. If we have spiritual content, we can minister to the saints through 1 Thessalonians and through the Gospel of John. No matter the book, we should be able to minister the spiritual content. What we should fear is not having spiritual content to minister to people; however, if we have spiritual content, we will be able to minister and develop any book of the Bible. Therefore, changing the way others do things indicates that we have not learned many spiritual lessons. It also indicates that we are inexperienced in the way we conduct ourselves.

Some brothers lead the saints to serve fervently, hoping that they can spend more time to learn to fellowship with the Lord and to know the indwelling Spirit. We should not change their practice. We should even praise them, saying that it is good to love the Lord and be fervent. However, our praise should not be insincere. It should positively supplement their labor. We always need to have an attitude of respect, cooperation, and coordination with others. We should serve according to our portion and honor the portion of others, because both portions have been entrusted by the Lord. Everyone should have the humility to not regard his portion higher than another person's. We should take care of others' feelings. Unless they speak heresy and create problems for the work and the church, we should always respect them, be accommodating toward them, and receive help from them.

May the Lord grant us grace to see that this is a matter of life that involves being broken and being humble. Those who can reach a goal without forcing others to take their way are truly humble. As those who love the Lord, we desire to live for Him and build up the church. These goals are right, but there are many ways to reach these goals. For example, preaching the gospel with a brother is a good goal that can be done according to his way or according to our way. We receive the blessing when we do not force others to do things our way. If we have spiritual content, we can minister his way, and if he has spiritual content, he can minister our way. Both ways are acceptable; it is not necessary to adhere to a certain way.

Preserving the Consciousness of the Body and Being Built Up in Our Service

The brothers need to learn the lesson of being broken, accommodating others, and respecting others' function. Our Lord is great, and His work has many aspects. Thus, we must be faithful to what the Lord has entrusted us with and learn to work in coordination with others, respecting what they do. Unless they speak heresy, we should not interfere, intervene, or criticize. Only in this way can we preserve the consciousness of the Body and produce the building among us.

The seeds of these problems are sown among us and have already produced some negative situations. Since we are serving the Lord together in His work and sharing this work together, we must rise up to utterly condemn such situations. These matters are intimately related to us and will manifest how much we have been dealt with before the Lord and the lessons of life we have learned. If we have grown in life, been broken, and learned some lessons, we will be saved in all these matters. When the elders suggested studying the Gospel of John and the responsible brother for the home meeting said that it was too long, insisting that the elders accept his way, the feeling of coordination was weakened. Once the feeling of coordination is weakened, we cannot expect the building of the Body to be strong.

If this brother continues to oppose the proposals of the elders, the brothers and sisters in his meeting will eventually rise up to oppose him, because he took the lead to oppose others and give his opinions. If he continues in this way, how can he lead the brothers and sisters in his home meeting to have a strong service in coordination and a good building? We all need to learn a serious lesson. In the coordination of the Body, everyone needs to function and respect what others do.

We should not criticize others but should join their labor so that the Body of Christ can be supplied, not damaged. In this way, the feeling of coordination in the Body will be sweet, and the building up of the Body will be strong.

CHAPTER THREE

NOT DOING A TEARING DOWN WORK IN THE CHURCH SERVICE

OUR SERVICE NEEDING TO PRODUCE THE BUILDING

The building of the church is carried out through the administration of the church and the ministry of the word, both of which depend on the condition of our person. Our administration of the church might not result in much building up of the church. It is also possible that our ministry of the word might not result in much building up of the church. Even our bringing people to salvation and helping the saints to be edified might not result in much building up of the church. Our work may be effective, but the more we work, the less there is the element of building. In other words, the effectiveness of our work is inversely proportional to the building up of the church. This is the tearing down of God's building work, not its building up.

Under normal circumstances, the more we work, the more we build. Our work should be our building. For example, when some preach the gospel, they not only save sinners but also build up the church; when they edify the saints, they not only help the saints but also build up the church. We need to take heed to this one thing: we may work without producing the building. If we are in the light, we will see that it is possible to save sinners and edify the saints without building up the church. Many works in Christianity are tearing down the work of God's building. The most serious tearing down of God's building in the church is not the result of persecution or opposition from the unbelievers. It is the result of the many zealous works in Christianity. These works do not come out of evil intentions, wicked thoughts, or errors. They have the good purpose of saving sinners and edifying the saints. However, they do not issue in the building up of the church.

SATAN'S SCHEME BEING TO DO A WORK OF TEARING DOWN IN THE CHURCH SERVICE

What does it mean for our work to tear down God's building? A good example of this occurs when a brother responsible for a group meeting changes the proposal of the elders to study a particular book of the Bible. While his changing the book may edify those in his meeting, the way he does it tears down God's building up of the church. It does not help the saints to know their flesh, deal with their opinions, or learn to submit to others. His way will only produce people with views and opinions, who like to adjust others and do not submit to others. Although this brother has a good intention and neither criticizes nor judges others, the destruction to the church is serious.

The elders may decide that the whole church should study the Gospel of John, but a responsible brother may think that this book is too long and change it to 1 Thessalonians. This good intention shows that he has not learned the lesson of being broken, he does not know how to put his opinions aside, and he does not know how to submit to others in the church service. The church cannot be built up if twenty-one responsible ones say, "The elders are not necessarily right in their way of doing things. Their decisions are not always correct." Once this attitude is adopted, things will get out of control.

These responsible brothers might not be satisfied even if the apostle Paul was one of the elders. Whether the elders make right or wrong decisions is not our problem. Our need is to submit to them. It is difficult to believe that one who does not submit to the elders can produce people who are broken, deny themselves, place themselves under God's hand, and submit to others. The best they can do is produce ones with views and opinions that tear down instead of build up the church.

To build up is to put one stone upon another stone. In contrast, the Lord's word in Matthew 24 shows the tearing down: "There shall by no means be left here a stone upon a stone, which shall not be thrown down" (v. 2). In tearing down, no stone is left upon another stone; in building up, every stone is upon another stone. People may praise our work, but we need to see if our work tears down the church. Satan's scheme is to tear down. All our work in Taiwan has been building up; however, during the past six months there has been much tearing down. This is the scheme of the enemy, and many among us have been used by him to do this work of tearing down. We do not want to do this work of tearing down. No brother or sister is doing this work of tearing down out of an evil intention. However, because we have not learned the lessons, we are unconsciously used by Satan in our service to tear down. Satan uses our work to tear down. We may think that we are building up, but our work is tearing down the church. Satan tears down through our work. This causes our service and the testimony of the church to suffer a great loss.

TEARING DOWN LEADING TO DISSENSION AND DAMAGING THE AUTHORITY IN THE CHURCH

We need to search our heart and consider whether our work during the past six months has brought us into one accord or into dissension. To be in one accord is to be building up; to be in dissension is to be tearing down. The responsible brothers are in dissension if they change the intention of the elders without the feeling of tearing down. If seven of the twenty-eight home group meetings are in this condition, the church in Taipei will be in discord and scattered.

We are not here to establish the authority of the elders as if they were popes, but we need to ask whether there is an administrative authority in the local church. In whose hands should this authority be? If this authority is in the hands of the one thousand brothers and sisters who meet regularly, we will become the church in Laodicea (cf. Rev. 3:14-22). If this authority is in the hands of a pope, we will become the Roman Catholic Church. The administration of a local church is in the hands of the elders. The elders should learn to submit themselves to God and fear Him. They should administrate the church in fear and trembling and learn to be strong. They should be afraid of making mistakes and of being weak and indecisive. If a group meeting should be stopped, the elders should make the decision without hesitation; otherwise, the remaining home meetings will become like small local churches.

If no one in a local church has been broken, fears God, or acknowledges the authority in the church in his service, that local church is in discord. Their many activities will result in more tearing down. It would almost be better to have fewer activities. If any of the responsible brothers in the church in Taipei have an opinion that differs from the decision of the elders, there will be a tearing down work in the church. Such a situation of dissension will cause death. If the responsible ones in the homes are like this, those in the groups will also voice their opposing opinions. This kind of trend can be likened to the body contracting an infection, which will kill the body. This is dissension and tearing down.

Through the subtle scheme of Satan, our labor may in fact be a tearing down work. Some brothers and sisters have made a great sacrifice for the Lord and for the church. On the one hand, we should not boast of the sacrifice we have made, but on the other hand, since we have made such a sacrifice, we should not allow Satan's scheme to enter into our midst. If we serve in discord, we will have no way to continue. Satan's most cunning scheme is to do a dissenting and scattering work in our midst.

Satan's work is not to cause everyone to argue; rather, it is to do a work of tearing down through man's good desire and intention. This is his craftiness. Apparently, the suggestion of the responsible brother to study a different book of the Bible is for the benefit of the saints, but in fact, it is not. However, if we have truly learned the lesson, we will see that although the arrangement in the church service should be flexible, not rigid, there must be one accord and one move in the church. In this way the church will avoid falling into Satan's schemes.

THE AUTHORITY OF THE HOLY SPIRIT IN THE BIBLE

Every local church must honor the authority of the Holy Spirit, whether it is large or small. For example, although thousands among the Jews had believed in the church in Jerusalem (Acts 21:20), there was not a conference of the church for the people to vote on different matters in chapter 15. Instead, the apostles and elders gathered together before God, and after some shared their experience and light, James stood up and spoke (vv. 6, 22, 13). This is the authority of the Holy Spirit in the Bible.

After meeting together, they wrote a letter to the Gentile believers (v. 20). They did not quarrel, nor did the church hold a conference for the believers to express their opinion through a vote; instead, the apostles and elders gathered together before God to decide the matter. Once they made a decision concerning the problem of circumcision, no further opinion was expressed.

NOT SOWING THE SEED OF DEATH AND DISSENSION

Those who have learned the lesson will say Amen when the elders decide that the group meetings should study the Gospel of John. Those who feel that this book is too long should be helped by those who have learned this lesson to submit to the church and respect the authority of the church. We must first help the saints to accept the arrangement of the elders before suggesting that a shorter book be studied. Helping the saints in this way is beautiful and contains the element of building in one accord.

If, out of an impure motive, a responsible one doubts the decision of the elders and shares his feeling with other responsible ones, the factor of death will be spread. He might not slander or oppose the elders, but in his speaking he may spread the thought of the church being a dictator. This will cause dissension. The seed of dissension that is sown into the saints can grow and eventually cause them to be in dissension with the church. This is tearing down God's work.

Even in our preaching of the gospel and our edifying of the saints there may be a factor of tearing down. This can be compared to drinking a cup of tea that contains the tuberculosis bacteria. After drinking the tea, we will contract tuberculosis. It is a serious matter if a brother, who did not possess a dissenting heart before being edified by us, begins to express an element of dissension in his service after being edified by us.

A local church is finished if all the saints are dissenting.

We must be aware of this great danger. The most cunning scheme of Satan is to sow the seed of dissension through the serving ones. When he does this, the work of the Lord is disrupted and there is discord in the church service. A person who has contracted tuberculosis may appear healthy, but within a year his entire being will collapse.

TO BUILD UP BEING TO MUTUALLY SUPPORT AND SUPPLY ONE ANOTHER

Our problem is that we consider ourselves to be so smart and capable that we do not need one another; we are always stepping on others. This is an indication of discord with the element of tearing down. This is not building up. Those who truly build up the church feel that they cannot act independently and cannot be without the brothers and sisters. They feel that they need others. When ministering the word, such a one needs the brothers and sisters to pray for him, to support him in their spirit. Such a spirit seems to have disappeared from our midst. Those who minister the word do not seem to need the prayer of others, and those in the audience do not have a supporting spirit. They just listen to the speakers and make comparisons. Such a spirit is intolerable.

When the seed of dissension that is in our midst bears fruit, then the church, our service, and the work will collapse and fall apart even though we may be more spiritual. Our labor has not brought people into one accord with the church. Instead, we seem to only be causing dissension. The more we help people, the more they seem to dissent from the church and are scattered. There is tearing down, not building up. In particular, the brothers and sisters who work with the young people do not have the feeling of depending on one another.

We should all be of one soul to pray for, supply, and support whoever is speaking a message. If those who serve the Lord are continually disagreeing, instead of being in one accord, the enemy, the saints, and even the children will know it.

BUILDING BEING SUBMISSION

Real building depends on submission. To submit is to be in subjection to others. When we are willing to submit, there will be the building. Submission is not an issue if only one person is working. But if we are working together, we must not simply care for our own work. For example, submission is not an issue before a brother and sister are married, but after they are married, they must learn to submit. Only when there is submission can there be building. When a brother and a sister are married, their purpose is to build up a family. The foundation of this building depends on submission. The emphasis of building is not on obeying but on submitting. If a wife does not submit to her husband and a husband does not submit to his wife, their family will lack the building. We must believe that the elders in a local church are not careless in their decisions and that they are not authoritarian in their attitude. Although they may feel that they are weak and inadequate, they bear a great responsibility and take care of the church in fear and trembling. If all the elders have this kind of attitude and spirit, their decisions are deserving of our submission.

LEARNING THE LESSON OF BUILDING AND BRINGING OTHERS INTO THE BUILDING

A person who argues about which book the church should study and doubts the decision of the elders does not have a submissive spirit or attitude. Without submission, there is no building. The building up of the church through our administration of the church and ministry of the word depends on our person. If we have learned the lesson, are broken, and know God's building, those whom we lead will be living stones being built up as a spiritual house. If we have not been built up, we have no way to build others up. The work in our hands will not result in building up. The more people we save through preaching the gospel and the more people we edify will only bring more opinions into the church. Even though the number of stones for the building increases, there will be no building.

Satan's work is to tear down. He has been doing this for two thousand years. Most of the gospel work in Christianity attracts people to believe by means of material gain. This is poor and superficial, and it shows that the power of the gospel has been lost. When a church is full of dissension, its condition will be weak. Since we came to Taiwan in 1949, the church in Taipei has been fresh without any dissenting factor. Satan is now attempting to do a tearing down work. When we are in one accord, we have the authority of the Holy Spirit.

BEING CAUTIOUS WITH OUR WORDS TO AVOID BRINGING IN DISSENSION AND TEARING DOWN

Some brothers are not cautious in their words, and they unconsciously bring in dissension and tearing down even though they do not have a bad intention. For example, a matter that was fellowshipped in the elders' meeting in the afternoon may spread throughout the church by evening, mixing facts with rumors. This shows that some brothers speak too much and have not learned the lesson in the church service. We do not have any secrets, but those who have been dealt with do not speak casually. For example, I recently sent out letters inviting brothers to come for a meeting, but I did not tell my wife. Eventually she received the news from another sister. If a brother receives a letter, he should simply come on the appointed date. There is no need for him to tell others about it. This kind of casual speaking is meaningless and gives room to Satan.

There is nothing secretive about sending out letters about a meeting. To not spread the news that you were invited to a meeting is to reject the flesh. I had a heavy burden to call a meeting, but I did not tell my wife about it. I could not even tell my wife about my burden, so why do the brothers need to ask my wife about it? This small matter can bring in dissension and tearing down. Those who have learned the lesson will not speak carelessly in their service and coordination. Although we may speak of many different matters with people, we must know our place when we speak of matters related to the service.

For the purpose of giving hospitality to Brother T. Austin-Sparks, I wanted to find someone who could cook Western food. We found a cook and paid him, but he ran away with the money. The next day a brother wrote a letter in which he offered to lend me his cook. I was surprised that the news spread so quickly. A person who has learned the lesson in service would never speak of such a thing. Even if one thousand cooks ran away, why is there a need to speak of it when it has nothing to do with us? This does not mean that the cook's behavior is a matter that must be kept secret for fear of what others may think. The Bible records that one of Paul's co-workers, Demas, loved the present age (2 Tim. 4:10) and that Paul exhorted the brothers in Ephesus, saying that he who steals should steal no more (Eph. 4:28). Thus, a cook running away with money is not a strange thing. But why would this news be spread in less than two days? This indicates that we need to learn the lesson of not spreading information. Spreading information tears down.

A brother once remarked that others were asking him if he was going to serve in Taichung, even though he was unaware of this information. This spreading of information occurred among the serving ones. Whether or not the brother was going to Taichung, it was not necessary to spread the information. If this brother needs to fellowship regarding his service in Taichung, he will come for fellowship. We do not need to ask so many questions.

If we want to build up the church, we need to let the Lord deal with us in these matters. Otherwise, the more we work, the more we will tear down and the more dissension will be produced. Many unnecessary words can be spread through the serving ones. We need to ask the Lord for His mercy. The serving ones should not speak carelessly. We need to learn this lesson. We may speak with the brothers and sisters about many different things, but in our service we should not be careless to speak of things that the Lord has not committed to us. In matters pertaining to our service, we should not speak so freely.

Some serving ones once spread the following word: "The elders cannot make up their mind on any matter. They are continually making changes and do not inform us of the changes." This shows that they have not learned to be restricted or ruled by the Lord. Although they may be consecrated to the Lord in their service, a few sentences can tear down a year's worth of work. They work with one hand and tear down with the other. This is not building. We need to be on the alert to see that the work in Taipei today is in discord and has fallen into Satan's scheme. Satan is spreading dissension through our serving.

If these problems are not dealt with, we will not have the building. The problems in the administration of the church and the ministry of the word are the result of the problem in our person. Please allow me to say a strong word: the spirit of insubordination is operating in our midst. Insubordination means tearing down, not building up. To be insubordinate is to not build, to not be built, and to tear down.

CONCLUSION

In order for our work to produce the building, many negative factors within us must be eliminated and dealt with. There are certain things we should not say, certain attitudes we should not express, and certain actions we should not take. In order to submit, we need to be restricted. Because those who are not restricted are unconscious of the many dissenting factors within them, there is a dissenting element in their words. We should not put the Lord to shame or come short of our consecration. Our work must build up, not tear down. It must be in one accord, not discord.

It is difficult to know how much breaking and restricting we need in order for our work to be in one accord and to build up others. Although these words are strong, please receive them with a humble and meek heart. We bear a heavy responsibility before the Lord. We will each give an account to Him at His judgment seat. If our work tears down, it will hinder many from receiving grace and being edified. This is a serious matter. We must learn not only to work but also to do a work that builds up. We should never allow our words, attitudes, actions, and expressions to produce any dissension or result in any tearing down in the church. We are not here to build up human authority; rather, we are here to build up the church of God so that His authority can be expressed in the church. Therefore, there are things we should not say, actions we should not take, and attitudes we should not express. These require us to learn before the Lord.

Chapter Four

THE SIGNIFICANCE OF BUILDING REVEALED IN JOHN 14

Scripture Reading: John 14

John 14 seems easy to read, and there have been many expositions of this chapter in the Bible, but this chapter is difficult to understand. Most people are short of proper light concerning this chapter. By the Lord's leading and our experience, we are beginning to understand the true meaning of this chapter.

This chapter speaks of God's building in the universe. The teaching of the Brethren has resulted in the mistaken consideration that John 14 is a chapter on prophecy. The Brethren consider the Lord's word in verse 3, a word spoken to His disciples before His departure from the world, to be a word of prophecy. They understand this verse to mean that the Lord Jesus was going to heaven in order to prepare a place for us and that once this place was prepared, He would come and take us to heaven so that we would be with Him. Hence, the Brethren determine this to be a chapter of prophecy. However, the thought in this chapter is richer, deeper, and higher than the thought of the Brethren. They do not see the true meaning of verse 3.

THE CENTRAL THOUGHT—
BELIEVING INTO GOD,
BELIEVING ALSO INTO THE LORD

In verse 1 the Lord said, "Do not let your heart be troubled; believe into God, believe also into Me." This verse is the subject of the chapter. The Chinese Union Version translates this verse as, "Believe in God, believe also in Me"; however, the word *in* is actually *into* in Greek. Hence, the correct translation should be, "Believe into God, believe also into Me." The Greek word for *into* is the preposition *eis*. This same word is used in the phrase *baptized into Christ Jesus* in Romans 6:3. This preposition means "to enter into." For example, if we have a box, and we squeeze our hand through a hole on one side of the box, our hand enters into the box. Therefore, *into* best conveys the meaning in English.

The central thought of John 14 is, "Believe into God, believe also into Me." As those who believe in the Lord Jesus, we need to believe *into* God and believe *into* the Lord. In reading the Bible it is very important that we grasp the subject. For example, Genesis 1 begins by saying, "In the beginning God created the heavens and the earth"; thus, the subject of Genesis 1 is God's creation. Likewise, John 14:1 says, "Believe into God, believe also into Me." Our need to fully enter into God is the subject.

THE LORD'S GOING BEING HIS COMING

In verse 2 the Lord said, "In My Father's house are many abodes; if it were not so, I would have told you; for I go to prepare a place for you." Verse 1 says, "Believe into God," that is, enter into God. Verse 2 continues with, "In My Father's house"; this is a marvelous turn. According to the natural understanding, the Father's house refers to heaven. However, the Bible says that the church of the living God is the house of God (1 Tim. 3:15). It does not say that the Father's house is heaven. What is this Father's house, and what does the Lord's going refer to? The erroneous understanding of the Brethren is that the Lord's going was His leaving the world to go to heaven.

In John 14:3 the Lord said, "If I go and prepare a place for you, I am coming again and will receive you to Myself." The Chinese Union Bible translates *to Myself* as "to the place where I am." Thus, people understand this verse to mean that the Lord will receive us to a place—the place where He is. However, He is not referring to a physical location. The Lord's word here means that He will receive us into Himself, not into a physical place.

"If I go…, I am coming" is according to the original text. The Lord's going is His coming. His going to prepare a place for the disciples was His coming to them.

GOD COMING TO EARTH THROUGH MAN, AND MAN BEING JOINED TO GOD THROUGH THE LORD

Verse 3 continues, "So that where I am you also may be." What does *where* refer to? The Lord was not referring to heaven but to the Father. He would be in the Father, and we would also be in the Father. The word *where* does not refer to a place. It refers to being in the Lord and in God. The Lord's going through His death and resurrection was not to be in heaven but to be in the Father. When the Lord was resurrected, He entered into the Father, and He also brought His disciples into the Father. This is the meaning of *so that where I am you also may be*.

In verse 4 the Lord continued, "Where I am going you know the way." The disciples were not the only ones who did not know where the Lord was going. Many of us also do not know. However, the erroneous teaching of Catholicism says that the Lord went to heaven to prepare mansions for us. This concept is not in the Bible. We, therefore, should not have the thought of going to a heavenly mansion. In verse 5 Thomas said to the Lord, "We do not know where You are going; how can we know the way?" This verse shows that according to Thomas's understanding, the Lord was speaking of going to a place. The Lord's reply, "I am the way," shows that He was not referring to a place. The Lord said, "I am the way and the reality and the life; no one comes to the Father except through Me" (v. 6). Because a literal translation of *no one comes to the Father* is not standard Chinese, the Chinese Union Bible translates the second half of this verse as: "No one comes to the place where the Father is except through Me." As a result, people consider that *the place where the Father is* refers to heaven or a heavenly mansion.

The phrase *to the Father* in verse 6 refers to believing into God, into the Father. This verse does not refer to our going to heaven through the Lord Jesus, but rather to our being joined to God and contacting Him. No one can touch God or enter into God except through the Lord Jesus. The Lord Jesus is the way, the reality, and the life; no one comes to the Father except through Him. Hence, it is altogether not a matter of going to heaven. According to the teaching of the Brethren, this chapter speaks of going to heaven; however, this chapter speaks of believing into God, not of going to heaven. There is a picture of a heavenly mansion with a ladder that refers to Christ. The picture also has the inscription: "No one comes to the Father except through the Lord." This implies that to go to the Father is to go to the heavenly mansion. This understanding is absolutely wrong. John 14:6 means that no one can enter into the Father except through Christ; no one can contact God except through Christ. Therefore, *where I am going* means that through His death and resurrection, the Lord was entering into the Father.

TO BE IN GOD BEING TO BE IN THE HEAVENLIES

Our human thought always conflicts with the thought of God. Our mind always considers going to a place—heaven or hell—but God's thought is a person, not a place. We think about heaven and earth; God thinks about God and man. The focus of the Bible is the Lord Jesus' entering into man, not His coming to the earth. The Lord Jesus' becoming flesh and entering into man is His coming to the earth. Similarly, man enters into God; he does not go to heaven. If the Lord Jesus did not enter into man, He could not come to the earth. In order for the Lord Jesus to come to the earth, He had to enter into man. In other words, when the Lord Jesus entered into man, He came to the earth. Similarly, man goes to heaven by entering into God; when man enters into God, he is in heaven.

Our human concept is related to a place, whereas God's concept is related to a person. As long as God can enter into man, He can come to the earth; as long as man can enter into God, man can enter into heaven. The earth is related to man, and heaven is related to God. If the God of heaven came to the earth without entering into man, it would not be considered His coming to the earth. He had to enter into man for His coming to earth to be complete. Likewise, without entering into

God, man cannot go to heaven. In order for man to go to heaven, he must enter into God. When man enters into God, he is in heaven. If we can grasp this thought, we will be able to understand the Bible.

Ephesians 2:6 says, "Seated us together with Him in the heavenlies in Christ Jesus." We can be seated together with Christ in the heavenlies because we are in Him. If we are not in Christ, we are on the earth, not in the heavenlies. However, because we are in Christ, we can sit with Him in the heavenlies. We may feel as if we are on the earth, but since we are in Him, we are in the heavenlies. We cannot be in heaven by being in ourselves; rather, we are in heaven by being in Christ. We need a change in our concept.

GOD'S HOUSE BEING GOD HIMSELF

Protestantism has adopted the thought of Catholicism and frequently speaks about going to heaven. Actually, we are in heaven; we have been seated with Christ in the heavenlies since the day we were saved because the day we believed into Christ, we entered into God. There is no scriptural basis for the teachings of Catholicism and Protestantism concerning going to heaven. Even Paul is not in heaven; he is in Paradise. We must understand that it is a matter of person—God and man. It is not a matter of place—heaven. God's entering into man is His coming to the earth; man's entering into God is man's going to heaven. For this reason the Lord Jesus said, "Where I am going you know the way" (John 14:4). He was actually saying, "I am now going to the Father. Just as I entered into man through My incarnation, I am now going to the Father to enter into Him through My death and resurrection." The disciples thought the Lord was referring to a place and replied, "We do not know where You are going; how can we know the way?" (v. 5). Then the Lord Jesus said to them, "I am the way...; no one comes to the Father except through Me" (v. 6). The way is the Lord Himself, and the destination is the Father. Hence, it is not a matter of place but of believing into the Lord, believing into God.

Through His death and resurrection the Lord Jesus brought man into God to enter into a union with God. When man enters into God, he enters into the realm of heaven, that is, the realm where God is. From this perspective, it is a matter of place. The beginning of chapter 14 speaks of God and God's house; God can never be separated from His house. One must enter into God in order to enter into God's house. Whoever enters into God has entered into God's house. Therefore, no one can enter into God's house apart from being in God. One must be in God in order to enter into God's house.

In His incarnation the Lord Jesus came from the Father and entered into man. However, for Him to go back to the Father, He needed to pass through death and resurrection. Through His death and resurrection, the Lord went back to the Father from man. Therefore, the Lord was going to be in the Father. This is where He was going. The Lord's coming was a matter of entering into man, not of coming to earth. His going was a matter of going to the Father, not of going to heaven (v. 28). The Lord entered into man through His incarnation, and He entered into the Father through His death and resurrection. The Gospel of John does say that the Lord Jesus ascended into heaven; it says, "No one has ascended into heaven, but He who descended out of heaven, the Son of Man, who is in heaven" (3:13). However, we should not say that the Lord's going to the Father refers to His going to heaven. The Lord Jesus did not go back to heaven. He was with the disciples, and He dwells in us all the time. Since He wants to dwell with us, how can He leave us? Therefore, the Lord's going in chapter 14 does not refer to His going to heaven; it refers to His going to the Father from man. "Believe into God, believe also into Me" is the subject of this chapter. The Lord Himself is the way for us to believe into God. The Lord entered into the Father through death and resurrection, and we entered into the Father through the Lord.

"If you had known Me, you would have known My Father also; and henceforth you know Him and have seen Him" (v. 7). The Lord wanted the disciples to know that it is not a matter of position or place but of a person, that is, the Father. Philip said, "Lord, show us the Father and it is sufficient for us" (v. 8). Jesus answered, "Have I been so long a time with you, and you have not known Me, Philip? He who has seen Me has seen the Father; how is it that you say, Show us the Father?" (v. 9). These words are very meaningful. These verses do not speak of a place; they speak of a person. They speak of God, not of heaven. It is a matter of entering into God, not of going to heaven. This chapter is not on the rapture or ascension. It is on the Lord Jesus bringing man into God through His death and resurrection. "Believe into God, believe also into Me" is the subject of this chapter. This matter is altogether concerning a person.

In verse 10 the Lord said, "Do you not believe that I am in the Father and the Father is in Me? The words that I say to you I do not speak from Myself, but the Father who abides in Me does His works." Whereas verse 2 says, "In My Father's house," verse 10 says, "The Father who abides in Me." Where does the Father dwell? Where is the Father's house? Logically speaking, the place where we dwell is our house; our house is the place where we dwell. Many Christians think that the Father's house is heaven, but verse 10 says, "The Father who abides in Me." This shows that when the Lord Jesus was on the earth, He was the Father's house. We cannot say that a person lives in Taipei but that his house is in Taichung. A person lives in his house.

THE LORD'S GOING TO PREPARE A PLACE BEING FOR THE ENLARGEMENT OF CHRIST

If the Lord Jesus is God's house, how can He go to prepare a place for us? His going to prepare a place is the enlargement of Christ. First Corinthians 6:19 says that our body is a temple of the Holy Spirit within us. First Peter 2:5 says that we are being built up as a spiritual house. Ephesians 2:21-22 says that we are growing into a holy temple in the Lord, into a dwelling place of God in spirit. First Timothy 3:15 says that the church of the living God is the house of God. *House* and *temple* in these verses refer to the dwelling place of God. The house is the temple, and the temple is the dwelling place of God. The dwelling place of God is a mystery in the universe. God's dwelling place is a matter of a person, not a matter of a place. God's dwelling place is the church, which is composed of the believers. The believers are the enlargement of Christ.

If we grasp this thought, we will understand what God is doing in the universe.

God dwells in the church, and the church is the house of God. Therefore, the church has the element of man and the element of God with the element of heaven. God is in the church, and heaven is also in the church. Although the church is on the earth today, it is heavenly, because heaven is in the church. Therefore, the church is the mingling of God and man, and it is the joining of heaven and earth. This is God's dwelling place. This dwelling place of God is different from His dwelling place in heaven. God's dwelling place in heaven is merely heaven; it does not have the element of man and is not joined to the earth. However, the church, obtained by God as His dwelling place, is a mystery, because God has entered into man and mingled Himself with man. When God comes, heaven comes, and because man is here, the earth is also here. This is the mingling of God and man, and it is the joining of heaven and earth. Although such an entity is not of the earth, it is on the earth. Although it is on the earth, it is of heaven and has the element of heaven. Such a dwelling place, the mingling of God and man and the joining of heaven and earth, is the eternal dwelling place which God is building. This is the place the Lord said that He would go to prepare; this place includes the church and heaven.

In John 14:11-12 the Lord said, "Believe Me that I am in the Father and the Father is in Me; but if not, believe because of the works themselves. Truly, truly, I say to you, He who believes into Me, the works which I do he shall do also; and greater than these he shall do because I am going to the Father." In these verses the Lord was saying that He would enter into the Father, and He would also bring those who believed into Him into the Father. Here there is a person as well as a place. Heaven can be expressed on earth because it is in God and is expressed through the mingling of God and man. This is a mystery. The element of heaven can be expressed on earth through the mingling of God and man. This is the New Jerusalem.

The New Jerusalem, like the church, possesses the mingling of God and man, and heaven is also mingled with it. The church is composed of the believers who are mingled with God and the condition, the element, of heaven that is also in us. In this way both God and heaven are expressed on earth. Even though this is a miniature, we cannot fully apprehend it. In the coming new heaven and new earth, the time of maturity and fullness, God will be fully mingled with man, and man will fully enter into God. God will take man as His dwelling place, and man will take God as his abode; thus, the elements of God and heaven will be brought into man and expressed on earth. This is what the Lord Jesus meant when He said that He was going to prepare a place for us.

BUILDING BEING GOD'S UNIQUE GOAL

We should not think that after God has saved all of us sinners and has finished building mansions for us in heaven, He will come and take us to live in these mansions. God has only one building work in the universe. In this work sinners are saved to become building materials that are then mingled with God. The element of heaven is also in this mingling. This is God's building, where God takes man as His dwelling place and man takes God as his abode. This is a mysterious abode; it is "the city which has the foundations, whose Architect and Builder is God" (Heb. 11:10). In the universe God has only this one work, this one building. In this building God is mingled with man, and heaven is joined to earth.

The entire Bible shows the building work of God. The completion of this building is the manifestation of the New Jerusalem. The New Jerusalem is God in man, that is, God taking man as His dwelling place. It is also man in God, that is, man taking God as his abode. Ultimately, God and man, man and God, are mingled together. God brings heaven into the New Jerusalem; the condition and element of heaven are in the New Jerusalem. Furthermore, the New Jerusalem is not only expressed on earth but also joined to earth. God and man are mingled together; heaven and earth are joined together. Man takes God as his dwelling place, and God takes man as His abode. This is the building of God in the universe. Even though this can be called a place because heaven is included and is expressed on earth, it is a person because God is in man. This is what God is building today; it is a city which has the foundations, whose Architect and Builder is God. This building is the place the Lord is preparing. Hence, Revelation 21:2 uses the word *prepared:* "New Jerusalem, coming down out of heaven from God, prepared as a bride adorned for her husband."

The goal of God's work is the building. He saves sinners and edifies the saints for the building. The New Jerusalem is composed of all the saved believers. According to Revelation 21, the city has a wall and twelve gates. The names of the twelve tribes of the sons of Israel are inscribed on the gates, and the wall has twelve foundations with the twelve names of the twelve apostles of the Lamb (vv. 12-14). God is not building a dwelling place with the intention of taking us there when it is complete. This is not according to the revelation in the Bible.

We are the house, the dwelling place, that God is building. We are God's temple, the dwelling place of God through the Holy Spirit. As living stones, we are being built up as a spiritual house (1 Pet. 2:5). In its completion the temple will be enlarged to become the city. Therefore, there is no temple in the city (Rev. 21:22). The city is the enlargement of the temple.

God's work today is to build a dwelling place for Himself in the universe. Hence, in speaking of the city, verse 3 says that the tabernacle of God is with men, and He will tabernacle with them. Saving sinners and edifying the saints are not God's goal. He saves sinners and edifies the saints in order to gain a building on the earth. God's building is a corporate man, not an individual person. This is His dwelling place.

John 14 shows what God is doing in the universe. Saving sinners and edifying the saints are only part of God's work. He is doing a building work. God wants to prepare a dwelling place. This dwelling place is a mysterious entity. It is God mingling Himself with man and working man into Himself. This building also includes the element of heaven; heaven is joined to earth. Hence, it is the mingling of God and man and the joining of heaven and earth. This is the work which God is doing today. If we understand this point as we read the New Testament, we will receive much light and will apprehend the meaning of the New Jerusalem and the church. We will also understand our goal and purpose in the Lord's work. We are not here simply to save sinners and edify the saints; rather, our goal is God's building, His dwelling place on earth.

God is doing a building work. The Gospel of John, Acts, and the Epistles show the stones for God's building. Acts 4:11 says that Christ is the cornerstone; Ephesians 2:22 says that we are being built together in Him into a dwelling place of God. In 1 Corinthians 3, Paul says that we are God's building (v. 9) and that we should take heed how we build (v. 10). "If anyone builds upon the foundation gold, silver, precious stones, wood, grass, stubble, the work of each will become manifest" (vv. 12-13). Hebrews 11:10 speaks of "the city which has the foundations, whose Architect and Builder is God." God is designing and building a city. According to verse 40, the Old Testament saints need the New Testament believers in order to receive God's promise.

Although Abraham was built by God, many in the New Testament age have not been built; hence, the city has not been manifested. However, the city will be manifested, prepared, and built by the end of Revelation. Revelation 21:3 clearly says that the New Jerusalem is God tabernacling with men. It is filled with the element of heaven, and it is expressed on earth. This is the joining of heaven and earth, the mingling of man and God. It is not the blessing of individual spiritual believers. God's temple becomes a city, God's dwelling place. This is what God wants and what He is doing. This is God's goal, His central work.

CHAPTER FIVE

THE ONENESS IN JOHN 17

Scripture Reading: John 17

THE PROCESS OF THE ONENESS

John 17 is the Lord's prayer in which He asked the Father to fulfill all that was spoken in chapters 14 through 16. In chapter 14 the Lord spoke of the coming Comforter; in chapter 15 He spoke of the vine, showing that our relationship with Him is like the union of a vine and its branches; and in chapter 16 He said that the unique factor in this union is the Holy Spirit. The Holy Spirit comes not only to convict us that we may have a union with the Lord in love but also to transmit all that the Father and the Son have into us.

John 17:1 begins with *these things Jesus spoke. These things* refers to the contents of chapters 14 through 16. After speaking the things in chapters 14 through 16, the Lord prayed to the Father: "Glorify Your Son that the Son may glorify You" (v. 1). The Lord prophesied that He would be glorified and that the Father would be glorified in Him (12:23; 13:31-32). In 12:24 the Lord said that He would die as a grain of wheat in order that the shell of His humanity could be broken and the divine life within Him would be released and dispensed into many people and expressed through them. Because this divine life is the divine element of God the Father, the Father is glorified in the Son through the Son's glorification.

The phrase *I am coming to You* in 17:11 confirms the Lord's words in chapter 14—that He was going to the Father and that His going was His coming. Hence, the Lord's prayer in chapter 17 reveals the significance of what was spoken in chapters 14 through 16. The Lord desired all His believers to be one even as the three of the Triune God—the Father, the Son, and the Spirit—are one.

Chapter 14 verses 20 through 24 say, "In that day you will know that I am in My Father, and you in Me, and I in you. He who has My commandments and keeps them, he is the one who loves Me; and he who loves Me will be loved by My Father, and I will love him and will manifest Myself to him. Judas, not Iscariot, said to Him, Lord, and what has happened that You are to manifest Yourself to us and not to the world? Jesus answered and said to him, If anyone loves Me, he will keep My word, and My Father will love him, and We will come to him and make an abode with him. He who does not love Me does not keep My words; and the word which you hear is not Mine, but the Father's who sent Me." These verses show how the oneness comes into being. Through His death and resurrection, His going, the Lord entered into God and brought man into God, making God man's dwelling place and making man God's abode. This is how the oneness came into being.

This oneness is the result of building, the result produced by the Lord Jesus' going to prepare a place. The preparation of a place is building; this preparation work is the work of building, which results in oneness.

ONENESS BEING THROUGH BUILDING

In a physical house all the materials are in oneness because they have been built up. This also applies to the spiritual building. If a brother is not experiencing the building, it is difficult for him to be one with the brothers and sisters in the church. A stone or a plank of wood must pass through building to become part of a house. Ephesians 4:11-13 shows that God gave apostles, prophets, evangelists, and shepherds and teachers as gifts for the perfecting of the saints unto the building up of the Body of Christ, until we all arrive at the oneness of the faith and of the full knowledge of the Son of God. The oneness is the issue of the building. The oneness is not merely a matter of having the same views and opinions. The oneness is a matter of being built up.

Before the Holy Spirit descended on the day of Pentecost,

the one hundred and twenty in the upper room were in one accord. They all continued steadfastly with one accord in prayer (Acts 1:14). Their oneness did not come instantly. Prior to praying in one accord, the disciples had received the Holy Spirit (John 20:22). This became a factor of their oneness, enabling them to pray in one accord. They had also been under His leading for three and a half years and had been taught by the Lord for a period of forty days after His resurrection (Acts 1:3).

The extent of building up determines the extent of our oneness. For example, even if the brothers and sisters in the church in Taipei have no opinions and do not disputes, we cannot say that this is oneness. Genuine oneness comes from being built up. There might not even be oneness among the serving ones. The absence of disputes does not necessarily mean that we are one. It is one thing to have no disputes, but it is another thing to be one. For oneness, we must be built up by God. For this reason, we cannot stay away from the church; we cannot stay away from the brothers and sisters with whom we are to be built up. A piece of wood may be good material, but if it is not built into a house, it is meaningless. Merely being good material is useless. Only when the materials are built into the house can there be the genuine oneness.

GOD'S BLESSING BEING IN THE ONENESS

God's blessing to the church is in the oneness. The Holy Spirit moves in the oneness, the power of the gospel is in the oneness, the authority of God is in the oneness, the light of God is in the oneness, and the supply of the divine life is also in the oneness. However, in order to have the oneness, there must be the building up. Without the building up, there is no genuine oneness. Even if there is a kind of oneness, it will not last. Only when we are built up can we have the genuine oneness. We may serve together without being one. We may not have opinions but still not be one. Only when we are built up can there be the oneness. We do not abound in God's blessing, and His presence is not evident among us, because there is not enough building among us. This is strong proof that we lack submission to authority.

We may not argue in our meetings, but we are not in one accord, because there is not much building among us. When the brothers and sisters come to the meeting, there is neither harmony nor coordination in their spirit. Even the serving ones are independent. This shows that we have not been built up.

We love the Lord and have risen up to pursue Him. Even though we may feel uneasy when we miss the meetings, this does not show that we have been built up. We pray when we are inspired and are silent when we are not inspired. We do not care for the condition of the brothers and sisters and are not bothered about being an isolated Christian. Although we are saved and come to the meetings, we are detached and isolated. Even the full-time serving ones are like this. When they come to a meeting, they are isolated and detached in their spirit. This causes the spirit of the meeting to be weak.

If the full-time serving ones are harmonious, coordinated, and in one accord, the meeting will be strong, rich, and full of blessing. This proves that God's presence is in the building up. Hence, the key to God's blessing and God's presence is in the building among the serving ones.

A car is a good illustration. When we step on the accelerator, the car moves because it has been "built up." If we only have separate car parts that are nicely painted, the car will not move, because the separated parts are not "built up." In the same principle, sometimes the serving ones in a meeting have been "taken apart." They are not coordinated; rather, they are independent, doing their own thing. This shows that the serving ones have not been built together. This makes it difficult for the brothers and sisters who are under their care to be built up. The result is that the prayers and activities in the meetings are independent and individualistic, not corporate and not in oneness.

A pile of good auto parts that have not been assembled or coordinated is useless. Because there is no building, there is no way for the car to move. In 1946 I labored in Shanghai and Nanking. Every time I went back to Nanking, I had a clear sense of one accord, whether it was in the singing, prayer, or the message. In the Lord's table meeting all the saints in the church in Nanking testified the same thing; they were our letters of commendation. Even those who went to the meetings occasionally felt refreshed.

Today I sense a loose spirit in many meetings. Every person is distinctly an individual. We function according to inspiration. We pray or call a hymn when we are inspired. However, we are disconnected and unrelated. Although we do not quarrel, there is no building. There is not only the absence of organic building; there is even the tearing down. For example, two brothers may coordinate well together, but after others join them, they are stumbled in their coordination. Since we are detached and lack the building, it is not easy to see God's blessing and presence in our midst.

It is not easy to see God's presence in individual spirituality. His presence is manifested where there is one accord, where there is harmony. Hence, in Matthew 18 the Lord said, "If two of you are in harmony on earth concerning any matter for which they ask, it will be done for them from My Father who is in the heavens. For where there are two or three gathered into My name, there am I in their midst" (vv. 19-20).

If there is no one accord among us, we cannot expect any blessing even if we labor diligently without quarrels or arguments. Others may achieve great success with little effort, but we have little success no matter how much we apply ourselves. Even if we have God's blessing, and our work helps others to learn in life, receive spiritual edification, and love the Lord, we will not be able to carry out an eternal work. Our work will not produce the building. It will not cause the saints to serve the Lord in love, being dependent on one another and making them His dwelling place. God does not want people merely to be saved and become spiritual. He wants the building.

If we have only edification but have not allowed God to do a building work in us, we may administrate the church as elders, but our administration will lack the element of building. Whether we are co-workers or those who minister the word, we will not produce the result of building. Our speaking may bring people to salvation and cause people to become spiritual, but it cannot produce something for the building. We may be able to gather much material for the building and work on it, but these materials will not be able to be built together with other materials. We may be able to visit people and help them to become spiritual, but there will not be any building.

May God have mercy on us to make us humble. We should not think that as long as we can save a few people for the Lord, we know how to do God's work. This is not what God wants. God wants a building. Where there is the building, there is the oneness; where there is the oneness, there is something genuine. This is what God wants.

DIFFICULTIES AND PROBLEMS BEING MAINLY DUE TO INDIVIDUALISM

There is a certain matter that causes my heart to ache. After hearing a brother speak, some have come to me and complained that he was attacking others in his speaking. When the brothers give messages, their purpose is to edify. Concerning the content of their messages, I do not believe the brothers say anything heretical. There is also no need for them to attack others when they speak. If we have a motive in our labor, we are not doing the building work. The saints are as simple as children. The brothers should cooperate with God to speak for God for the purpose of building, not for tearing down. The brothers who minister the word should not help on one hand and transmit germs on the other hand. Otherwise, the saints will be edified and harmed at the same time. This will issue in the tearing down of the building.

After listening to a message given by a young brother, some have come to me and asked about his speaking. This indicates that there is a thorn in his work that makes people feel uncomfortable. We may think that we have done a work yet be unaware of a thorn in our work. This kind of work is not helpful. Our messages should not attack people; they should be positive. Our speaking should give life. It should not cause people to make negative comparisons or have a critical or judgmental feeling. The goal of our speaking is the building up. Therefore, we should not give the saints the impression that our speaking is higher than that of others. Instead, the saints should have the impression that our speaking is in harmony with the speaking of others. The saints should not feel that one brother is attacking another brother when he gives a message. Although the brothers speak from different angles, they are one. Hence, we must endeavor to speak words of building. This requires us to be broken and built. Otherwise, it will not be possible for us to do God's work. This is a solemn matter.

Although the local churches stand on the proper ground, the situation among the churches seems to be one of self-government. We should not have local flavors; rather, we should have only the flavor of Christ. For example, if we come to Kaohsiung we should sense that we are simply the church in Kaohsiung. A believer can only be in one locality, and he should be for the building in that locality.

However, this can cause another problem if a local church is unwilling to fellowship with other churches. When different localities were being raised up by the Lord, the brothers did not know how to administrate the churches, and they relied on other local churches. For example, the churches in Tainan and Kangshan depended on the church in Kaohsiung. After making some progress, they began to take care of themselves without depending on Kaohsiung. Although they do not quarrel, argue, or dispute with the church in Kaohsiung, they practice self-government. Those in Kaohsiung may be able to break the bread with them, but there is a feeling of independence. There is not even the building among the individual saints. The lack of building among the local churches is the result of a lack of building among the saints.

The brothers who do the young people's work do not depend on one another for life. This is very disappointing. They are clever and capable and feel that it is more efficient to work alone. This type of individual labor, however, will not have any result. Although they may not quarrel or argue with others, they are unable to get along with others and serve the Lord together in one accord. Hence, there is no blessing.

We cannot deceive others concerning our true condition. When others touch our spirit, they can know our true condition and are clear whether we are being dishonest. The responsible ones for the young people's work have an uncooperative spirit. They say that they need others and that they cannot be independent; however, in their hearts, they wish that they did not have to work with others.

If we want to have the Lord's blessing and His presence, and if we want others to be edified, we need to learn to be built up. We must do one work in the position, atmosphere, and spirit of being built. Only then will our work produce the result that God seeks and blesses. If we have seen this light, we will prostrate ourselves before God and say, "I cannot live independently of others. I need to be built regardless of how spiritual I am."

BUILDING SOLVING ALL THE PROBLEMS IN THE CHURCH AND BRINGING IN GOD'S BLESSING

Paul was the greatest apostle of the Lord. Nevertheless, when he wrote the Epistle of 1 Corinthians, he said, "Paul, a called apostle of Christ Jesus through the will of God, and Sosthenes the brother" (1:1). Paul's reference to Sosthenes shows that he had a consciousness of the Body and a spirit of coordination. It is doubtful whether many people have paid attention to the name of Sosthenes.

The apostle's spirit is different from ours. The isolation among us is becoming more serious. Everyone is capable, the younger ones and the older ones, and it seems as if there is no need to depend on one another. The older ones think that they are more experienced and know everything concerning the administration of the church. They feel that they know how to be elders. Even though they might not say this, it is the attitude in their spirit. We can be polite and call this a spirit of tearing down, but it is actually a spirit of rebellion. When a brother speaks, some may be critical and say in their heart, "I know this already." This kind of spirit is destructive to God's work.

We should not expect our work to be blessed if we are isolated and individualistic. We should not expect such a work to produce the building. Since we minister the word and participate in God's work to some extent, there will be some results.

Even the work of the Catholic Church produces some results. We must ask, however, whether this work is producing what God wants. Can the Catholic Church edify two or three million people so that they are in one accord, love one another, and stand for God? The people they edify will be full of opinions. God is not able to build in them. He cannot gain a dwelling place, a habitation, in them.

By the Lord's mercy, may we see that we need to be built and labor in a work that builds up others. When we bring people to salvation, there must be an element of building. When we bring people to salvation, we not only need to make them spiritual, but we also need to build them up. After being led to the Lord by us, they should not only love the Lord but also be built up with others. In the same principle, the elders not only need to administrate the church, but they also need to build up the church. Then the brothers and sisters under the elders' administration will be in one accord and will be willing to submit to others, considering submission as their glory. This is the glorious work that we need to do here.

Capacity alone is not the only measure. Compared to the elders, some younger brothers may be keener in terms of skill and mental capacity. But this does not mean that they can serve as elders. The qualification for being an elder does not depend on skill or mental capacity but on being broken and subdued. It is possible for our service as elders to produce saints who are dissenting and rebellious. Our service may save people and cause them to be spiritual and love the Lord zealously, but they will not be built up. Please allow me to say a solemn word. Since the beginning of the year I have felt that Satan wants us to do a work that is spiritual and full of zeal but which tears down and is lacking in mutual submission.

Many young brothers have been poisoned in this regard. We need to proclaim a warning. Those who desire to serve the Lord must take the way of building. If there is edification but no building, this is the way of rebellion. If there is spirituality but no building, this is the way of Satan. Throughout the two thousand years of church history no person was useful in God's hand who was unwilling to put himself under God's hand and be subdued. The work God desires today is not only to save sinners or edify the saints. The primary work of God is to build a dwelling place.

We should never think that the building is not essential or can be easily "manufactured." God must do much work in order to build up an isolated person. He wants us to enter into glory. He wants us to be built up with others into His glorious dwelling place. Unless we are coordinated and built up with others, we cannot enter into glory. If we can coordinate, God will add others to us who can also coordinate. If God cannot build in us today, He will still do it later. Those who enter into God's glory must be built by God.

In order to be built, it is crucial that we are able to coordinate with others. In order to coordinate with others, we need to be broken. We may consider ourselves to be an excellent stone but be unable to be built up. Likewise, we may consider someone who is able to coordinate with others to be an ugly stone. This only shows that being able to be built with others, not spirituality, is what matters.

It is not easy for God to find a group of people who is willing to be subdued and built up by Him. God wants to pour out His blessing, but it is not easy for Him to find such a vessel. The Lord said that if two or three are gathered in harmony, He will be with them, and their prayer will be answered (Matt. 18:19-20). In other words, God's blessing is wherever the building is manifested. If one-tenth of the serving ones in Taipei are in one accord, God's blessing will follow their service. On the contrary, even if there are no arguments in a locality, if there is no building, God's blessing will not be present. God's blessing is based on our one accord, being in harmony in spirit with one another, having real coordination, and having genuine oneness. For example, if five brothers and four sisters meet together, the brothers should be submissive toward one another just like the sisters. If a brother chooses a hymn, everyone should sing together with rejoicing. Such a condition and spirit will bring in God's blessing.

PRIDE INVITING DESTRUCTION, AND HUMILITY BRINGING IN BLESSING

There is also much pride in our midst. It is painful to hear the questions: "Why is he an elder, and I am not? Why is he leading the whole church, and I am leading only a group meeting?" This is pride. Pride is a source of suspicion, and it causes a person to think that the elders highly regard others but not him. This is shameful.

If this is our condition, we may be able to give wonderful messages, but our work will have no result. The primary matter is our person, not the way we speak. The ability to preach better than Paul will not make our work more effective. Everything depends on our person. A proud person will bring forth others who are proud. We bear fruit according to our kind. We reap what we sow. One who ministers the word with pride should not expect to reap the fruit of humility. One who administrates the church with pride should not expect to reap a church of humility. If we administrate the church with pride, it may rise up to condemn and even reject us.

The presence of such conditions among us gives us a heavy burden. We must see what God is doing in the universe. Someone might proudly say, "Behold! All of these have been saved through me." We may have led many to salvation, but they may all be sick, because we are sick. In this way we damage the church and have no way to prevent the spread of our sickness. Those who love the Lord will not praise us for our work. If we hope to be equally loved and praised by those who love and praise the Lord, we will reap the fruit of our labor one day.

In Matthew 7 the Lord said, "Many will say to Me in that day, Lord, Lord, was it not in Your name that we prophesied, and in Your name cast out demons, and in Your name did many works of power? And then I will declare to them: I never knew you. Depart from Me, you workers of lawlessness" (vv. 22-23). In these verses *never knew* means "never approved." The Lord did not approve what these ones did. Therefore, we should always ask ourselves whether our preaching the gospel is for the building and whether our administration of the church is for the building.

We may think that we are competent in administrating the church, but after three years the church will be in rebellion. May the Lord have mercy on us to see that the spirit of Babel is rebellion, which is intolerable. If we can humbly receive mercy, we will be blessed. May the Lord have mercy on us to deliver us from the spirit of Babel that we may be humble and submissive.

The seed of pride within all of us is the greatest problem to the Lord in His building work. This is the source of our lack of building. If we want to be built, we must submit to others and accommodate them. Submission requires humility; accommodation requires meekness. A person who is neither submissive nor accommodating is proud, feeling that he can do everything by himself.

LEARNING IN SERVICE—
BEING HUMBLE IN RELATION TO OURSELVES
AND PURE TOWARD OTHERS

There is no position in serving the Lord. We should not expect others to exalt us. A brother once said that if those who serve the Lord were respected, many would rise up to serve the Lord. This is wrong. On the contrary, when the Lord's servants are despised, a multitude rises up to serve the Lord.

In our service there is no such thing as position, and we should not covet position. We should not expect to be highly regarded or appreciated. We should be prepared to be ill-treated without any appreciation for our labor. Our reward is not from men.

This, however, is not our situation. Formerly we were clear that our pathway was contrary to the world. We were clear that this was not the pathway for those who desire glory. We should not say that those who serve the Lord should be respected in order to attract others to serve the Lord. Such an atmosphere proves that we are in degradation. Even if we are not respected, others will continually rise up to serve the Lord; they cannot be stopped.

We must realize that everything is of God and that He bears full responsibility. God has led us to walk this way. This is His doing. We cannot stir others up or control them. It is shameful for someone to use financial means to control others or even to control the Lord's servants.

The Lord wants us to see that all the work depends on Him. The way we are treated by others is secondary and should not bother us. Those who serve the Lord need to be prepared to place everything in His hands and live only to Him. God bears full responsibility for our needs. We live by faith even if we must make tents like Paul (Acts 18:3; 20:34).

We need to be humble and pure as we serve. To be humble is to put ourselves aside and submit to God's arrangement. To be pure is to acknowledge that everything comes from God; we have no motives or expectations. We take this way whether people praise or oppose it. When we are appreciated, we take this path; when we are not appreciated, we still take this path. We take this way whether others agree or disagree. Walking on this pathway is altogether a matter between God and us; it has nothing to do with anyone or anything else. Those who serve the Lord should be like this.

Toward the end of Paul's ministry, he said, "All who are in Asia turned away from me," and "at my first defense no one was with me to support me, but all abandoned me" (2 Tim. 1:15; 4:16). It seems that Paul was saying that many received his ministry, but no one stood with him at his first defense. Nevertheless, the Lord stood with him and empowered him so that through him "the proclamation of the gospel might be fully accomplished" (v. 17). In our service we should not desire to win the sympathy of others. Our way is in the Lord.

All those who serve the Lord need to be humble in relation to themselves and pure toward others. They should not long for sympathy from the brothers and sisters, and they should not expect a high position, nice treatment, compliments, or positive responses. We must be pure in our goal of seeking only God. We must also be humble and submit to others and to our circumstances. We serve the Lord and those who love Him. If the Lord could wash the disciples' feet, who can we not serve? If the Lord could go to Hades, where can we not serve? Whether we serve in a large or small locality and whether we serve as elders to administrate the church or only clean the restrooms, we need to endeavor in our service. Only in this way can we do the work of building. This kind of service will produce an organic result of building. Otherwise, our service may only produce "giants." Please remember that we reap what we sow.

Satan is doing a subtle work to cause us to be individualistic and in discord even though we do not argue. Hence, we work with one hand and tear down with the other. In such a situation it is difficult for us to have the blessing; it is difficult for our work to produce an organic result. God's blessing is on the one accord and the oneness. Genuine oneness comes with the building. If we are built, we can be with the brothers in any locality, under any circumstance. Whether we are an elder or sweep the floor, we will serve with thanksgiving and praise. We will be flexible in our coordination.

If we learn this lesson before God, our serving as elders will result in the building up of the church, and our cleaning the meeting hall will also result in the building up of the church. Then no matter which book the elders want us to pursue, whether it is the Gospel of John or the Epistles to the Thessalonians, we will have no preference. As long as we are those who are being built, no matter where we are placed or what we are asked to do, we are in the building. Everything depends on whether we are being built by the Lord, not on whether we are asked to minister the word.

The full-time serving brothers do not earn their livelihood by preaching; rather, they are those who have sacrificed their future to serve the Lord. May we be those who are in the Lord's heart and learn to receive His breaking. May we say as Sister M. E. Barber said, "Lord, I have no other desire than You."

THE GENUINE BROTHERLY LOVE BEING THE BUILDING

Another reason for the lack of building among the serving ones is that we are short of love for one another. This shortage of mutual love causes my heart to ache. There is no genuine love among us, and we do not care much for one another. It seems as though we are satisfied with merely getting along with one another. It is as if we are merely colleagues. Without brotherly love, however, we will lose the testimony and the Lord's blessing.

There should be an extraordinary love among the serving ones. This is a crucial point in John 13 through 17. The Lord's word to us and His prayer for us was to love one another (13:34;

15:12, 17). Such a love for one another comes from our oneness with the Lord, and it is not something ordinary. This is to love one another in the Lord's divine life and in the Lord's love (17:26). Only this kind of love can build us up.

CHAPTER SIX

BUILDING UP IN LOVE AND KNOWING PEOPLE

John 13:34-35 says, "A new commandment I give to you, that you love one another, even as I have loved you, that you also love one another. By this shall all men know that you are My disciples." The words *know that you are My disciples* can also be rendered "know that you are those who follow Me." John 17:21 says, "That they all may be one; even as You, Father, are in Me and I in You, that they also may be in Us; that the world may believe that You have sent Me." Verse 23 says, "I in them, and You in Me, that they may be perfected into one, that the world may know that You have sent Me and have loved them even as You have loved Me." When people in the world see the oneness of the serving ones, they can believe that the Lord was sent by God, that He is the Christ of God. This oneness is the oneness of the Triune God.

The above verses show that harmony in love is the characteristic of those who are built up by God. When people touch this characteristic, they can sense that these people are followers of Christ. The characteristic of loving one another, the harmony in love, causes people not only to know that we are the Lord's followers but also to believe that the Lord is the Christ. In John 14 through 17 the Lord spoke of loving one another. If we study these chapters carefully, we can know the meaning of loving one another.

LOVING ONE ANOTHER

A believer who has not been built up by the Lord will not have genuine love toward people. A new believer loves the brothers and sisters. Although this love is of the Lord, it is a love at the beginning stage and cannot last, because it is not the love spoken of in the Gospel of John. In the Gospel of John love is an issue of a person's abiding in the Lord, fellowshipping with the Lord, and being one with those who belong to the Lord. Those who have been built by God have such a love.

Paul was one who had been dealt with by the Lord and built up by God. His love toward all the churches, the brothers, and the co-workers did not come from his natural emotion, his good intention, or from having the same temperament as others. The love that Paul had came from his being built up in the Lord. This love is seen in his Epistles through his words, attitudes, and actions, whether toward the churches, toward the individual believers, or the co-workers, and whether through rebukes or praise. He had an anxious concern for all the churches. If a co-worker, church, or saint was weak, he also was weak. If they were stumbled, he was sorrowful and indignant over the cause of their stumbling (2 Cor. 11:28-29).

LEARNING TO BE CONCERNED ABOUT OTHERS

Even though our situation is better than that of those in the world, there is a sense of love and concern among the serving ones that is lacking. Someone may like a certain brother and have much coordination with him, but this is not love. The Lord desires that we love one another even as He loves us. The Lord's love toward us is not based on emotion. He does not love us because we are worthy of His love. We are not lovable, and we do not treat the Lord in a way that is deserving of His love. If we deserved His love and treated the Lord well, we might be deserving of love, but such a love could be based on emotion. However, there is nothing in us that deserves to be loved; hence, the Lord's love toward us is not based on emotion. He loves us because we need His love.

There should be this kind of love among those who serve together and among the brothers and sisters. We should not love the saints because they are lovable. We should not love a brother because he is nice to us. We should love the saints because they are our brothers and sisters and because we have been dealt with by the Lord; we have been built up by the Lord.

We do not need to exhort the saints to love one another. The more building there is among us, however, the more the characteristic of love and concern will be expressed. Then our administration of the church and our ministry of the word will produce results. The brothers and sisters will love others also. Whether or not the brothers and sisters can love others depends on the administration of the church and the person of those who minister the word. Giving a message on loving one another might not be effective, but our administration of the church can cause the brothers and sisters to love one another. Sometimes the more we speak about loving one another, the less the saints love one another.

In some churches those who minister the word never speak concerning love, but the saints love one another. The elders might not lead the brothers to love one another, but under their administration the brothers and sisters spontaneously love one another. This happens when the brothers who administrate the church have been built up by the Lord. There is something in them that is concerned about others, loves others, and cares for them.

Let me give an illustration. A brother in the workers' home was sick for two days, but none of the other brothers visited him. The four brothers who normally eat breakfast with him did not seem to notice that he was missing. They may have thought, "I am not the one who is missing. I will eat my breakfast and then take care of my business." Can such a person serve the Lord? One who has been built by the Lord must learn to be concerned about others. If there is the genuine love, the four brothers will immediately check on the condition of the brother who is missing. This is the proper thing to do.

If we notice that a brother's socks are worn, we should find out if he has another pair. If he does not, we should get another pair for him without letting him know who gave it to him. This is to love one another. We have become degraded if we lack this kind of love for one another. It is useless merely to give appealing messages. If we observe that a certain brother always wears the same shirt, we need to find out whether he has any other shirts. We must have this kind of concern for others.

If we do not have such a concern, it is difficult to serve the Lord. We may be able to administrate the church in an orderly manner, but there is no building up in our administration. We may also be able to give messages, but the saints will not be built up. Knowledge puffs up, but love builds up (1 Cor. 8:1). However, this does not mean that we should give messages on loving one another; rather, we must be dealt with and built up by the Lord. Then we will be concerned about others and love them.

When we purchase a pair of shoes, we should consider whether the brother who serves with us has another pair. We should also have this consideration when we purchase new clothes. Sadly, this is not the situation among us. We should not take care of only our own living; rather, we should also take care of the brother beside us. This is a great and solemn matter. Someone once accused me of using money to control others. Such a word is an insult to me and to the brothers. The Lord knows that I have no intention to control the brothers. My only desire is for the needs of the brothers to be met. None of the brothers who serve should have needs in their living.

Simply giving things to others is not an indication of love. It can be a matter of emotions only. We should have a love that is concerned for others and cares for them. If a brother is sick or a sister has a problem, we should feel as if we are the ones involved. We must always think of the needs of our brothers. When we buy a pair of shoes, we should think of our brothers' shoes; when we have a suit made, we should think of our brothers' suit. We need this kind of consideration.

We should not think that it is a loss to care for those who serve with us. Even if we incur a loss, it is glorious. One who cares only for himself is quite poor; the poorest person is one who cares for himself the most. On the contrary, one who learns to care for others is rich. If we care for others and bear their burdens, we are rich. We should not bear merely our own burden. We should learn to also bear the burdens of

BUILDING UP IN LOVE AND KNOWING PEOPLE 75

others. By the Lord's mercy we should be able to testify that the more we bear others' burdens, the more the Lord bears our burdens and strengthens us. We should not be ones who serve the Lord without caring for those who serve with us. If we care for those who serve with us, our ministry of the word and our administration of the church will be able to build up the saints.

If an elder desires his administration of the church to bring in the building, he must learn to love and care for people. During one conference, there was a flu going around, and many people were sick. One of the brothers who did the cleaning was sick with the flu. I did not see him for several days. When I found out that he was sick, I went to visit him. When I saw him, I learned that no one had been taking care of him, not even those who shared the room with him. He was lying in bed with a fever and did not even have a cup of water. My heart was saddened when I saw the situation. If we are all like this, we do not need to speak or listen to any more messages, because they are useless. This brother was lying in bed with a fever, but everyone was indifferent to him. If a person who is indifferent becomes an elder or ministers the word, he can edify the saints but not build them up. Edification is for the benefit of an individual; building up causes the saints to be built up together. God does not want to gain individual persons; rather, He wants to gain a building. God cannot use work that has only individual results. Our work must produce a corporate result in order for God's will to be carried out.

A brother might not be able to give dynamic messages, but when he administrates the church, the saints are blended and built up. This is the church. The church is a corporate, built-up entity. The gathering of several thousand people is not the church if they live independently and are not built together. God has no building among them.

God needs the building, a corporate building. When brothers and sisters serve and meet together in love, their gospel preaching will be prevailing, and many will be brought to salvation. In some meetings, however, the brothers and sisters lack power when they preach the gospel. There is no sense of building with them; there is only a sense of desolation and dispersion. A church in which the brothers care for one another has a future. When our concern comes from the Lord's building work within us and not from exhortation, we have the building. If the serving ones do not care for one another, we should not expect our work to result in the building.

Our love for one anther is not an emotional reaction. Our love for one another should not be the issue of being nice to one another. When you are not sick and have no problems, I may not come to your room for two months, because you do not have a need. However, when you are sick and in need, I will definitely be by your side. If we genuinely love one another, we will be concerned no matter what our problems may be. There is genuine love for one another when we are concerned for each other. This is the issue of being worked on by the Lord. The more a person has been worked on and built by the Lord, the more he is concerned for others, cares for others, and loves others.

Dead and lifeless things do not need love. In a house there is no need for the wood to love the bricks or for the bricks to love the tiles, because they are dead. However, living things must love one another to stay together. In some localities even though the brothers are together, they are in discord and lack mutual love. There is no building among them. Roommates who live in the same room and do not argue may still be in discord if they have not been built. This is a sad situation.

It is very sad when we only notice a brother's new socks but not his worn socks. The normal condition should be that we do not notice when a brother purchases new socks, but we notice his worn socks. If this is our condition, we can do a solid work. We need to love the brothers and sisters and care for them, but such a love should be based on their need, not our emotions. When they have a need, we have a need. We should learn to bear their burdens (Gal. 6:2). Then the administration of the church and the ministry of the word will bring much building to the church.

The building of the church is not an easy matter. Bringing people to salvation and edifying them is easy, but building up the church is not that easy. Bringing people to salvation and edifying them do not require us to learn lessons. However, in order to build up the church, to build a group of people together, we must learn lessons. For the elders' administration to build up the church and for the ministry of the word to build up the church, we must pay attention to the points above. If we do not learn these points, we should not expect our administration of the church and our ministry of the word to build up the church.

Some people think that the elders should be humble and careful and that those who minister the word should be cautious with their words. This may be correct, but being humble, careful, and cautious is not what is important. These qualities will not cause the brothers and sisters to have a high regard for us, much less to be built up. Rather, their being built up depends on the practical points we have considered. We need to learn these points and be equipped with them.

LEARNING TO KNOW PEOPLE

It is also crucial that we learn to know people as we administrate the church and minister the word. We need to know people for the administration of the church, and we also need to know people for the ministry of the word. If we do not know people, we cannot build up the church; rather, the church will be brought into confusion and torn down. A person who wants to build up the church must know people. He must know the condition of the brothers and sisters. This includes their intentions before God, their flesh, and their spirit. Every skilled construction worker must be knowledgeable about stones, tile, and wood. He must be able to discern the nature of wood, knowing whether it is soft wood or hard wood. If he does not know the nature of wood and uses it indiscriminately, the houses he builds will be dangerous to live in.

Much of our knowledge of people is according to the dealings we have received. If the Lord has dealt with us in a certain aspect, it will be easier for us to know people in that aspect. If our motives have never been dealt with by the Lord, it will be difficult for us to see whether others are pure in their motives. If our intentions, motives, and purposes have been thoroughly dealt with by the Lord, when we touch others, we will know their intentions, motives, and thoughts, and we will immediately know the source of their problems. We will know when they are pure. If our flesh has never been dealt with and we have never learned the lesson of being broken, we will not know when others are in their flesh. Therefore, our knowledge of people is based on our knowledge of ourselves. Those who are serious and correct in their dealing with themselves will know people accordingly.

It is very important for the elders who administrate the church to know the intentions, motives, and purposes of the brothers and sisters. The elders need to know the spiritual condition of the brothers and sisters and where they are before God. When the elders do not know the brothers and sisters, they can make many mistakes. When someone who is courteous, eloquent, knowledgeable, zealous, and able to give messages comes to the church, the elders may think that he can serve in coordination. But when he is brought into coordination, an entire service group may collapse.

The elders who administrate the church must avoid fickleness. It is inappropriate for them to constantly change their evaluation of the brothers. They should not say that someone is spiritual and then change their mind two months later. This kind of thing must be avoided in the administration of the church. This can be avoided only by knowing people and continually learning to know people.

The elders who have learned this lesson and who have been dealt with by the Lord will have a clear knowledge of others, knowing where they are and the condition of their spirit no matter how they conduct themselves. You will know whether a person's speaking represents the real condition of his spirit. You will know whether he is filled with the uncleanness of the self and the natural man, because his spirit has never been delivered from the self.

You will know whether he would carry out a work all by himself. A believer may be experienced, knowing how to conduct himself, but not be delivered from the self. If his views and knowledge are worldly, he cannot have a spiritual service. If such a person becomes an elder, he will tear down the church even if he can minister the word. Any responsibility and coordination in service that he bears will be a tearing down work. It will be the same as installing a time bomb in a building; at a certain time the bomb will explode, and the entire building will collapse. Arranging for him to be an elder will result in tearing down, not building up. Instead of being good for the building, he will be like a time bomb. When it is time for him to lose his temper, the whole situation will be out of control. He may be able to gain people and befriend them by his humility, knowledge, eloquence, and persuasive speech, but this is all according to the flesh. The church will be ruined in his hand. This is the real situation in some places. Making a mistake in knowing a person can damage five years of labor. Some damage cannot be recovered in a short time. The Lord may require five years to begin a new work.

Some people pray according to their own leading, not according to the leading of the Spirit. Others speak according to their own leading, not according to the leading of the Spirit. We should not encourage such ones by giving them responsibility or a position in the service. We cannot forbid people from speaking in the church meetings, but we must observe them and see if their ways are proper. If their ways are improper, we should exhort them so that they know that their ways are not encouraged or approved. This will give them some feeling. We should not excommunicate them for speaking something improper, but when they do so a second time, we should tell them that their ways are improper. We need to give them the feeling that their ways are not approved. This will afford them the proper help.

When the elders do not have this kind of awareness, they may assign an older brother who seems humble, knowledgeable, and experienced some responsibility in the service. Afterward, when problems arise and the church is damaged, they will begin to realize that they should not have known people according to the flesh. This has been the situation in many places.

Discerning Man's Motives

If our judgment concerning people is inaccurate, our administration of the church will result in tearing down. A lack of knowledge concerning people will only cause the church to suffer loss even though we have no intention to tear down the church.

If we want to know people, we must learn to discern whether their motives and intentions are pure before God. If someone does not have a pure motive, we should not give him any responsibility in the service. Our knowledge of people's motives is based on the Lord's dealing with our own motives. If our motives have never been dealt with by the Lord, we should not think that we can know the motives of others. If our motives have been dealt with and are pure, our ministry of the word will not produce "side-effects" or result in mixture. Rather, we will be single and pure toward God.

We need to deal with our motives in all things, not only in the ministry of the word. When we learn this lesson, we will be able to easily discern the motives of those who come to us. After our motives have been dealt with, we will be able to easily discern the motives of those we meet. We may not be able to sense the purity in their heart, but we will immediately recognize the filthiness within them. We will be able to discern whether someone is single and pure or whether he is filthy in his motive. We can easily know a person.

Discerning Man's Flesh

A person whose flesh has never been dealt with or who has never learned any lessons concerning the flesh can never coordinate in service. We may allow him to serve, but we should not assign him to any service. This would be a mistake. Since it is difficult to find a person whose flesh has been absolutely dealt with, we should not assign people to any service unconditionally. In other words, a person's assignment in a service should match the degree to which his flesh has been dealt with. The more his flesh has been dealt with, the more we can assign to him in the service. If he has had little dealing, we should not assign him much responsibility in the service; this can lead to problems.

Suppose a brother loves the Lord, is zealous, and wants to serve. We should not rejoice when he expresses a desire to serve and allow him to participate in the service. This will not issue in the building. No one builds a house in this way. A carpenter must first look at his material in order to know the nature, condition, and size of the material to use in the building. Only then can he build. He must first assess the condition of the materials and then assign the materials according to their nature and condition; only in this way will his work be proper for the building.

However, the elders in some local churches are not like this. They rejoice when they see a brother who loves the Lord and immediately make him responsible for a group meeting. But since his motive is impure and his self has not been dealt with, his "tricks" all become apparent within a few weeks. Even though the saints may be fond of him, just as the children of Israel were fond of Absalom, the church will suffer a considerable degree of damage. Sometimes the damage cannot be recovered for several years, and the church suffers a great loss.

This affects the ability of a church to preach the gospel with power, the ability for brothers to be raised up, and the lack of vitality in the meetings. The entire church seems to suffer from poisoning, giving people the feeling of helplessness. This is the issue of the elders not knowing how to administrate the church and not knowing people. They are like a carpenter who does not know his material. Thus, it is difficult to have the building.

It is not difficult to preach the gospel and bring people to salvation, and it is easy to minister the word to edify people, but it is not so simple to build others up. For this reason the apostle Paul says, "As a wise master builder I have laid a foundation...Let each man take heed how he builds upon it" (1 Cor. 3:10). It is truly not easy to build the church. We cannot simply let the brothers and sisters grow on their own. We must see that the church needs administration and that a large part of the administration depends on our ability to know people and to discern their motives and their flesh.

Discerning Man's Spiritual Level

To discern a person's spiritual level is to know whether or not his spiritual condition is rich, strong, high, and pure. For example, there are some brothers whose heart is pure and whose flesh has been dealt with, but because their spirit is very weak and cannot rise up, they cannot do anything.

Concerning our knowing of people, we need to know man's motives, flesh, and spirit. Of course, there are some other points that we should also know, but these three are the most important. Assigning a person responsibility in the service according to a knowledge of these three points will result in the proper building.

A person who ministers the word and speaks for the Lord must know people according to their genuine condition in order for his words to move them. If we do not know people according to their genuine condition, we cannot know their true need. Sometimes a brother may give a message that is directed to one person because he feels uneasy speaking directly with the person. This is giving a message to rebuke a brother instead of ministering the word. Those who hear the word will know that the brother is being rebuked, and the brother himself will know. This is not proper.

Sometimes one person in the audience represents the saints as a whole. For example, there may be some who do not have the key to prayer, and one of them may be in the audience. Having been dealt with by the Lord in this area, we can release a message on the key to prayer. In this way no one will feel that we are speaking about a particular person. Although we are clear that we are speaking to him, our word will touch everyone because everyone needs such a word. If the message is strong, the brother will be among the first to testify that he was touched. Such a message comes from knowing people.

We should not speak to God's children without knowing them. This kind of speaking is empty and does not touch them. God's children do not need such messages. They do not benefit from our messages if we do not know them. This is a big problem. Our messages will hit the mark when we know people. If we want our messages to hit the mark and to be powerful, we must know people. If we want to know people, we must learn the lessons.

If we have never been dealt with in the matter of prayer

and do not have the key to prayer, we will not be able to know when others need a word on the key to prayer. A lack of knowing people makes our messages impractical. If we want our messages to be practical, we must know people. This requires us to learn every day.

The elders who administer the church must continually study to be able to discern the condition of others, know people, and discern the motives, flesh, and spirit of others. A person who ministers the word must learn how to sense the needs of others. None of the Epistles in the New Testament were written by first receiving God's revelation and applying it to certain needs. Rather, all the Epistles in the New Testament were written after first touching people's need and then receiving a word from God to meet that need.

Both Epistles to the Corinthians were written in this way. Paul was able to write because he saw the problems and knew the condition of the church in Corinth. This also applies to giving messages. Unless we know or observe the brothers and sisters, we will not be able to speak. Those who minister the word must know the genuine condition of those who listen and bring their situation before God. Brother Nee once spoke a message particularly to one elder. When we spoke of that brother's problem, Brother Nee told us that the entire Lord's Day message was spoken for him. If we want our administration of the church to be for the building, we must know people. The sisters who visit other sisters and fellowship with them should do so based on their knowledge of the problems and conditions of those they visit. This requires us to learn various lessons in a serious way.

CHAPTER SEVEN

THE BUILDING OF THE CHURCH REQUIRING AN ABSOLUTE CONSECRATION

In the administration of the church and the ministry of the word we need to know people in order to have the building. In addition, we must pay attention to the matter of consecration.

CONSECRATIONS THAT ARE NOT THOROUGH GIVING RISE TO PROBLEMS IN THE SERVICE

Everyone knows about consecration, but not many are clear concerning how consecration affects us. The problems that some serving ones are having may be related to consecration. We are not referring to material offerings. Consecration is a basic need for God to do a building work on the earth through us. However, this is not empty doctrine; it is a personal and practical matter. The improper conditions manifested among the serving ones indicate that their consecration is not thorough or is weak.

All our problems, difficulties, and sufferings are related to consecration. The more ease and comfort we desire, the less consecrated we need to be. If we do not want any sufferings, there is no need for consecration. We should not blame the Lord for giving us sufferings. Our sufferings are the result of our consecration. Some say that our sufferings are given to us by the Lord. In fact, the real sufferings of Christians are brought by Christians upon themselves. If we do not want any sufferings, we simply should not consecrate ourselves. We can be zealous, preach the gospel, and even minister the word without being consecrated. In Christianity we may be successful without having any sufferings. Natural disasters and man-made calamities are the portion of every person. A person who is not consecrated, however, is exempt from a large amount of suffering.

It seems as though the apostles in the early church life sought sufferings. If they had not been absolute and had compromised, they would not have had much suffering. If they had compromised, they would not have been persecuted by the Jewish religion and the Roman Empire. The sufferings that they experienced were the result of their consecration. They created sufferings for themselves because of their consecration. The sufferings the apostle Paul experienced were the result of his consecration. It would have been possible for him to love and serve the Lord without suffering any hardships if he had not been so absolute in his consecration. Paul said, "I now rejoice in my sufferings on your behalf and fill up on my part that which is lacking of the afflictions of Christ in my flesh for His Body, which is the church" (Col. 1:24). Paul consecrated himself willingly. He said, "I travail again in birth until Christ is formed in you" (Gal. 4:19). Paul's willingness came from his consecration.

BEING UNABLE TO DO THE WORK OF BUILDING IF OUR CONSECRATION IS WEAK

In contrast, our situation seems to reveal that our consecration is continually getting weaker. We may be excellent Christians and excellent preachers in the eyes of the world. Nevertheless, we cannot do the genuine work of building up the church, because our consecration is weak. When we consecrate ourselves absolutely, the saints sometimes do not approve. They would rather that we compromise in our service, that is, that we be moderate, neutral, or less than absolute in our service.

If we want others to welcome us, we only need to compromise in our service to the Lord. At least seventy percent of the saints will support us if we serve in this way. However, if we would be absolute in our consecration continually, those who support us will decrease and our suffering will increase.

In the apostolic age the apostles were persecuted wherever they went, but today few preachers are persecuted. This is not because the age has changed or because the world is more favorable toward Christians. Rather, the consecration of those serving the Lord today does not match that of the early apostles. The so-called serving ones of the Lord today have lost the consecration of the early apostles. If all the serving ones today consecrated themselves like the early apostles, they would experience many sufferings and hardships.

Many young saints are building up relationships with the view to entering into marriage and establishing a family; this is absolutely necessary. However, what we have observed causes us to wonder whether these relationships strengthen or weaken their consecration. We cannot condemn the young saints, but they should consider whether their consecration has been strengthened or weakened. Perhaps they are considering the future of their service, their burden, or their function. But do these considerations indicate a strengthening or a weakening in their consecration?

BEING UNABLE TO CARE FOR GOD'S HOUSE AND CARE FOR OUR HOUSE

Some Western missionaries once confronted me, saying that the brothers who are responsible for the group meetings should take proper care of their own households and not be in so many meetings. Although these brothers had a good intention, we should ask, "Whose house is more important, God's house or ours?" This is a matter of consecration. We cannot say Amen to the attitude that the Western missionaries have toward their families. Instead of sacrificing their households for the Lord's household, they sacrifice the Lord's household for theirs. We cannot say Amen to this. Perhaps their families are wonderful, but what is the condition of the church they lead? Almost all the saints who serve the Lord have families. If they would spend all their time with their families, producing families that are like happy gardens and children who are like angels, God's house would be gone. This is a matter of consecration.

If our consecration is absolute, even our children may rise up to oppose us. None of the children of the Western missionaries oppose their parents, because the missionaries care too much for their families. Some of them did not have servants in their own countries, but when they come to China, they hire someone to cook, someone to take care of the children, someone to do the laundry and cleaning, and a gardener, a driver, and even a guard. If we are truly consecrated, the first ones to oppose us will be our children. For this reason, I question the consecration of the missionaries who speak irresponsibly and sarcastically. Even though they are God's servants, we should not learn from their way of living. It is undeniable that we should do our best to care for our families. However, we also need to be clear concerning consecration.

A certain responsible brother has five children, and the group meeting he is responsible for has over a hundred saints. If he only takes care of his family, he cannot take care of the one hundred brothers and sisters. If he only takes care of the one hundred brothers and sisters, he would not be able to take adequate care of his family. It is difficult to know how to take care of the group meeting properly while adequately caring for his family. Taking care of the group meeting requires one's whole being. We even need to consider the group meeting in our dreams.

If we imitate the Western missionaries in how they care for their families, the result of our labor in the church will match theirs. At critical moments they say, "Brothers, I can no longer do this work because I must be with my children." We, however, cannot do this because of our consecration. May God bless us so that our families will receive mercy and care. However, we must be warned that the way of some missionaries is not our way. They do not take the way of consecration.

BEING UNABLE TO SERVE
BOTH THE LORD AND MAMMON

Brother T. Austin-Sparks once said that there are some problems with the Western missionaries in organized Christianity. We acknowledge that they traveled to a distant land for Christ's sake, but this does not mean that all the missionaries who came to China sacrificed and consecrated themselves. I have no intention to condemn their lifestyle, but we must know that the way of consecration results in many sufferings. Before we consecrate ourselves, we do not have many problems with our studies, jobs, or families. But once we consecrate ourselves, there are many problems. Before we consecrated ourselves, we may have been good teachers, doctors, civil servants, parents, or children, but the more we consecrate ourselves, the less capable we become and the more problems we encounter. In a sense, the One who troubles people the most is Jesus; He has "wrecked" innumerable people. Many talented ones have been wrecked by Him; many good students, good professors, good fathers, and good mothers have all been wrecked by Him.

When I was in Manila a group of young brothers and sisters asked me to speak to them. My first sentence was, "Jesus wrecks people." The young people in Manila need to be wrecked by Jesus, and the Christian families of the overseas Chinese in Manila need to be wrecked by Jesus. Do not think that our work in Southeast Asia is welcomed by people. Over the past few years we have been fighting the battle every day.

When I was in Manila in 1955, on one hand, the brothers there respected me, regarded me highly, and treated me well, but on the other hand, I was in a battle with them. I was fighting the battle concerning "heaven." I wanted to eradicate the concept of "heaven" from the core of their being. I told them that as Christians we should not think that being a Christian is a matter of asking for blessings, longevity, peace, of fearing the Lord, and of not sinning. Neither is it a matter of going to heaven to enjoy eternal blessings when we die. Such a gospel may seem very attractive, but this is altogether a religious concept that considers Jesus to be a person who is more trustworthy than a Buddha.

Therefore, I was strong in fighting the battle concerning going to heaven. I showed them the Lord's word in the Gospels: "If anyone comes to Me and does not hate his own father and mother and wife and children and brothers and sisters, and moreover, even his own soul-life, he cannot be My disciple" (Luke 14:26). This strong word touched the heart of those who love the world.

In a love feast I fellowshipped about how to read the Bible and pray, to receive grace and an answer to our prayers, and to be shown mercy by the Lord. A brother asked why I did not speak this way to all the saints but rather spoke of forsaking everything for the Lord and consecration. I immediately responded, "Dear brother, do you need me to give messages that even you can give?" After the meal I said to the elderly brothers that they needed to consider their condition. They should not simply say that the young people love the world and have no reality; rather, they need to consider their condition. When they saw me later, they were ashamed. Those who love the world should be ashamed.

Hence, whoever believes in Jesus will be wrecked. Everyone who has genuinely believed in Jesus is wrecked by Him. He is not corrupted by Him but wrecked by Him. If the young people want to follow Jesus, they will have problems at their schools. If one is a doctor, he should not expect to prosper. Most of those who live a smooth and prosperous life have problems with their consecration. A person who is able to prosper as a doctor, make money as a businessman, become famous as a professor, be recognized as a top student, or be an excellent father must have problems with his consecration. A person can serve only one master. If he is occupied with his studies, he will not have room for Jesus, and if he is occupied with Jesus, he will not have room for his studies. Similarly, if he is occupied with his children, he will not have room for Jesus, and if he is occupied by Jesus, he will not have room for his children. Therefore, it is impossible for a person to serve the Lord properly and also be a good doctor or a good father in the eyes of the world.

It is not difficult for a person to be well respected as long as he does not consecrate himself. However, this does not mean that those who serve the Lord and preach the word should behave unbecomingly. We need to conduct ourselves in a manner that is respectable and worthy of man's praise when we serve the Lord and preach the word. If we want to be absolute in our consecration, we must be prepared to live a life of sufferings. This price is set before us, and we must count the cost.

In these days the enemy is not only doing a dissenting work among us, but he is also leading many to weaken their consecration and be compromising Christians. We cannot serve the

Lord on one hand and belong to the world on the other; we cannot be successful in both. If all the serving ones would take good care of their careers and families, they would be more successful in their careers and they could take better care of their families. This can be compared to taking care of a garden by weeding and watering it every day. Such a garden surely will be beautiful. If a person manages a hospital and labors diligently every day, that hospital will surely be successful.

This is similar to the matter of consecration. If we devote ourselves to care for our careers, studies, and families, we should not expect the church to flourish. Instead, the church will be desolate and deserted. If we give our careers and families priority and put the Lord and the church in second place, the church will have no increase.

Meeting every day may cause us to suffer certain personal losses. But we must ask ourselves concerning the purpose of our existence. Are we here for our house or for God's house? A Western missionary in Manila testified that his oldest daughter and second son wanted to be preachers. He rejoiced that many of his children were preachers and that his family was a family of missionaries. If we live a comfortable and easy life and do not pay a price to follow the Lord, our children will want to follow us. Such preachers can travel around the world, have servants, suffer no lack, and be highly regarded by others. How many people can live the kind of life they do? If they took the way of a Nazarite, it is unlikely that their children would still want to be preachers.

Because those who serve the Lord in China have taken the way of consecration, none of their children have desired to serve. If we want to do a work of consecration and to take the narrow way in the Lord's recovery, we should not expect that there will be a comfortable life ahead of us. We cannot trust the way of the Western missionaries. If we take their way, we will do a work of Christianity, not the work of building up the church. When we do the work of building up the church, our fame, reputation, family, energy, and natural man will be wrecked. Our reputation and what we are will be wrecked.

Those who desire to serve the Lord and maintain respectability in their family, career, and studies have taken the wrong way. There is no way for us to be successful in both. If we want to allow the Lord to build and gain something, our consecration must be absolute. This is not merely a matter of following our parents or husbands because we have a desire to preach. This is a matter of being wrecked by Jesus. He will wreck our everything. This is a matter of genuine consecration.

However, this does not mean that we do not need to study, have a career, or take care of our family. We should not abandon everything. We should and must do our best in our studies, in taking care of our family, and in working. However, when there is a conflict between the two, we should ask which side should win. Should the Lord Jesus win the victory, or should our own benefit win the victory? We should also ask which side has the highest priority within us. What is our primary occupation? We should all have a definite answer before the Lord. Do we regard the Lord Jesus and His work as primary or secondary? If we want to do a work of Christianity, we can regard what pertains to us as primary and what pertains to the Lord as secondary. If we want to build up the church, we need to give the Lord priority.

SEEKING HELP FROM OTHERS
TO REDUCE OUR SUFFERING BEING A SHAME

The way of consecration is a way of suffering, a way of sacrifice, in which everything that pertains to us is wrecked. Some people consecrate themselves in order to gain sympathy from others and reduce their suffering. These believers have lost their consecration. It is shameful to seek help from others in order to reduce our sufferings. Those who are consecrated should learn not to seek help from others. We would prefer to suffer before the Lord than to seek help from others, and we would prefer to starve for three days than to let others know our need. However, this is not our situation. Some who suffer just a little desire to be noticed by others and to receive help from them. This indicates that their consecration is not as strong as it was in the past.

The first group of serving ones among us did not seek help

from others. They even told people that they would not take the way of receiving help from others. They had the ability to make money in the world, but for the Lord's sake they did not go to the world. This was the situation and character of the serving ones in the beginning. Sadly, some of us are now afraid that we will not receive help. It seems as if it is a shame for us not to receive help. However, it is glorious for others not to take care of us, because we serve the Lord full time. It is not glorious to seek the help and sympathy of others; rather, it is shameful.

We will become pitiful parasites if we always expect others to help us. Because of this, some are able to rebuke us, saying that we are the parasites of society since we depend on others for our living. This indicates that our consecration is not strong. However, this does not mean that the saints should not love or care for the Lord's serving ones. For many years the senior co-workers have held the principle that we do not appreciate or feel grateful for the care we directly receive from others. We do not want to receive any help directly from man's hand. Those with a burden to care for us should give through the offering box. We want to receive our supply directly from God's hand.

Someone once asked a full-time serving brother how much support he received that week. Such questions are an insult to those who serve full time. Such people should be looked in the eye and told that it does not concern them. Their questions do not reflect a love for those who serve the Lord; rather, they are an insult. A person who is truly concerned should put something in the offering box without asking how much a serving one receives. Such questions are improper.

The wife of a serving brother once said that her husband received only a few dollars a week. This caused others to feel that we should help this brother find a job. This is shameful. Since this couple was willing to take this way, they should not complain. One who serves the Lord should not be like this.

Those who take this way should be clear that this is a way of suffering and poverty. They should not expect to have a prosperous life. The Lord never said that those who take this way will have food to eat and a good living. Instead, He said that we should forsake our all to follow Him. We should even lose our life. This is the way of consecration. It is glorious if we can live by faith for an entire year without anyone showing concern for us. However, there are situations in which serving ones ask others for help. When we are in this condition, we can do the work of Christianity, but we cannot do the work of building up the church. When we build up the church, our fame, reputation, being, and family will be wrecked. Our reputation, what we are, and what we have must be buried. The apostle Paul was wrecked by the Lord; the Lord gained his everything. The Lord Jesus can wreck people. Many lives have been wrecked by Him. This is a matter of consecration, of paying the price; this is to "fill up...that which is lacking of the afflictions of Christ...for His Body" (Col. 1:24).

THE WAY OF CONSECRATION
BEING CONSIDERED AS ABNORMAL

We must consider this matter of consecration and consider the price that we must pay. Those in Christianity do not take this way. We must be prepared to be wrecked by Christ. We should not measure things according to natural thoughts. We should not consider our profession, marriage, family, or studies according to natural thoughts. The situation of the early apostles, the Christians in the early church life, and those who have followed the Lord throughout the ages surely cannot be considered as normal. We can be considered as normal only if we are not consecrated and not taking the way of consecration. All of the ways of consecration surely are abnormal. For example, the parents of Sister Dora Yu sent her to England to study medicine. However, when the ship she was on arrived at the port of Marseilles, France, she told the captain that she had to go back to China to preach the gospel. This is abnormal. We cannot take a normal path in our human life. If we take a normal path, we cannot take the way of consecration. May we all see that the way of serving the Lord is a way of consecration. Nothing is normal in this way; instead, everything is abnormal.

Chapter Eight

THE BUILDING UP OF THE CHURCH REQUIRING KNOWLEDGE OF DIFFERENT MATTERS

THE IMPORTANCE OF KNOWING MATTERS

In this chapter we will consider different matters that we should know. For the building up of the church, we must know people and different matters. If we simply want to be zealous ones who preach the gospel to save sinners and speak the truth to perfect the saints, there is no need for us to have a knowledge concerning various matters. However, in order to build up the church, we should know people and matters. We need to know those whom we contact and those who desire to serve the Lord. We need to know their motives, whether their flesh has been dealt with, and their spirit. We also need to know the nature, outcome, relationship, and impact of these matters.

There are many aspects of the things we need to know. For example, a brother who loves the Lord may say that the Lord has moved him to give ten thousand dollars to the church. On the one hand, we should thank the Lord and rejoice that this brother is willing to be used in this way by the Lord. On the other hand, we should realize that this is not a simple matter. We need to have some understanding related to the matter of giving. This means that we should understand the motive, nature, method, and purpose of the brother's giving. We also need to know the possible results and influence of his offering. If we simply thank the Lord and accept the offering, our work is not for the building up of the church; rather, it will tear down the church.

We must seek to be enlightened by the Lord through prayer and consideration in order to examine the history and background of the person who is giving the gift. We should consider his reputation and standing in society and the source of the money he is offering. We should also consider his intentions before the Lord and the spirit of his giving. When the elders receive a large sum of money as a gift to the church, they must take the time to understand how such a large sum of money was obtained. Moreover, they must seriously consider the potential effect, directly or indirectly, of the offering. In other words, the elders need a basic knowledge concerning this matter.

Suppose another brother says that he wants to offer fifty thousand dollars to help the brothers in poverty. Although this is good, it is not so simple. We should not simply thank the Lord for this brother, thinking that this is a timely offering to help the saints in need. We should not think that simply by distributing the fifty thousand dollars to the poor the church will be built up. On the contrary, we need to consider whether the offering can cause the church to be torn down. This can be compared to a surgery that causes a person to lose his life instead of healing him or to food that causes a person to become sick rather than nourishing him. In order to build up the church, we should not be simple persons. We need to learn to fully understand the situation we are facing. Then we can determine what we should do and how we should do it.

Discerning matters is related not only to the administration of the church but even to the ministry of the word. We may give a message to discourage instead of a message to encourage if we lack knowledge concerning a certain matter. Hence, if we want to learn to build up the church, we must learn to discern matters. We must learn to know every matter that is directly or indirectly related to the church, as long as it is something we can inquire into and something we can touch. Our ability to administrate the church depends on whether we are able to know people and matters. Our ability to preach the word and work for the Lord depends on whether we know people and matters. Even our ability to visit and help people depends on such knowledge.

Some responsible brothers act inappropriately in the administration of the church because they are short of knowledge concerning different matters. Some messages may edify the saints but result in tearing down rather than building up. This is the result of an inadequate knowledge concerning matters. A lack of knowledge can also cause us to tear down the church while we are building it up.

TAKING CARE OF NEEDY SAINTS

Two Western brothers, one of whom was a doctor, were among us for a period of time, but their work was not very profitable. They had a desire to serve with the saints, but we felt that they did not obtain much profit; neither did they render much profit to the brothers and sisters. The lack of profit was not related to edification but to the building up of the church. In relation to the building up of the church, we felt that receiving them into the service would result in a great loss. As those who serve the Lord, we should not gossip or be careless in our conversations about this matter. It is a fact, however, that our contact with these two brothers gave rise to many problems instead of the building up of the church.

According to our realization, problems could arise because we did not fully know what kind of persons these brothers were. We also were not certain what they were able to do or what would be the result of their work. Those who contacted them were confused and unclear. They helped many saints medically for no charge and even paid hospital expenses for some saints. However, all their work resulted in some tearing down of the church, not a building up.

One day my wife and I went to visit the brother who was a doctor. On the way we saw a sister whose child had contracted tuberculosis and had been operated on twice by this brother. The sister felt that it was the Lord's mercy that this brother had charged her only half the fees the first operation and performed the second without charging her. On the one hand, this brother was kind and took care of the poor. On the other hand, the ones he took care of were grateful to him but did not gain more Christ. Hence, it was not for the building up of the church. Furthermore, those whom he helped were not uplifted in their person; instead, they felt that they were inferior to this brother and to the responsible brothers. For this reason, what this brother did in love was actually a tearing down of the church, not a building up.

If this brother had a burden to help the saints materially, he could still accept medical fees and be led by the Lord to put something into the offering box. In this way the brothers and sisters would receive help directly from God's hand. They would not have a feeling of being debased before men; they would not feel that they had received help from man or even from the church. They would simply feel that God had visited them. This would build them up with a noble character.

If our help causes the brothers and sisters to feel inferior or indebted to us, we are tearing down the church rather than building it up. Our help should not cause others to feel grateful to us. In other words, they should not feel inferior to us. They should not feel that they are our beneficiaries. If we give people such a feeling, we are a charitable organization, not the church. The saints should not merely feel grateful to us, the church, or the elders. We must lead them to Christ; only this results in the building of the church.

If we maintain an attitude of giving alms, showing pity, or assisting the poor saints, we are corrupting the Lord's church. Although the sister whose son had contracted tuberculosis repeatedly thanked and praised the Lord, her entire being was corrupted. In her debasement, she became reliant on others and even subservient to them. Those who always receive help from others cannot be built up in their character, and the church cannot be built up. In this matter the two Western brothers truly needed our fellowship. However, we were unable to help them in this matter. This proves that we have no discernment concerning matters. Moreover, because of this, our work here cannot build up the church.

When we take care of the needy brothers and sisters, we must consider whether our care is for their building up or for their tearing down. This depends on our ability to discern things.

RECEIVING HELP FROM GOD AND NOT FROM MAN

We should not be indebted to others. We should receive our help from God, not from man. The past one hundred years of Christian work here has not built up the church; instead, it has damaged and torn down the church. The Western missionaries need to learn the lesson of helping people before the Lord without making them their beneficiaries. People should feel that they have received their help from God, not man.

It is not edifying for the Western brothers to give people the feeling of being their beneficiaries. By so doing, they make themselves superior to others. This will never build up the church. The church has been corrupted. When we help in secret, our help will benefit others.

NOT CONSIDERING OTHERS SUPERIOR AND OURSELVES INFERIOR

The Western brothers had good intentions, but they needed to consider their way. Their way was inappropriate because it did not edify. Many of the brothers were associated with them for a long time, considering that everything from the West was good and helpful. We never thought that we should help them in this aspect because we considered ourselves to be inferior. We should not think too highly of ourselves, and we should not consider ourselves inferior. We do need the supply from the West in many areas, but this does not mean that everything from the West is correct. This depends on our ability to discern matters.

We have received help from the Western brothers, but they also need to receive help from us. We should be humble and receive help from them, but this does not mean that everything they have is proper. We criticize them because we hope that we can all learn the lesson. When the elders decide to study a particular book of the Bible, they would not insist on another book if they were experienced in spiritual matters and in their behavior. These brothers were competent in their medical field, but in administrating the church and in touching spiritual matters, they were infants learning to speak.

Whether we can supply the need of the church does not depend on which book of the Bible we study. We can supply the spiritual need of the saints through any book. These brothers were not responsible ones in the church, but they gave the saints a negative impression. Before they rendered a supply, they adjusted others; before their capability was manifested, they criticized others. This indicates a lack of learning in spiritual matters and an inability to get along with others. Such a lack damages the building work of the church. Therefore, we need to learn to know people and discern matters.

When we are learning to serve the Lord, we must be able to discern matters. We should not think that everything from the West is good. We have invited Western brothers with great expectations, but the result of their visit causes us to be fearful. On their side, their conduct was inappropriate; on our side, we did not know how to express ourselves. We received many "Western meals," but the Western brothers refused to receive "Chinese meals." This is pride.

It is necessary to discern matters for the building up of the church. If we always appreciate the things of the West and despise the things of the East, the church will never be built up. The Lord is not only the Lord of the Jews; He is also the Lord of the Gentiles. Likewise, the Lord is the Lord of the Westerners and of the Chinese. He does not give light only to the West. Hence, while we should not be proud, we should not feel inferior. We should study whether a matter is right or wrong and whether it is helpful or not. We should not think that everything from the West is good and therefore should be received. Rather, we should learn to know people and discern matters.

As we are building the Lord's church, we must learn to discern matters. We should not treat anything lightly. We should carefully consider and evaluate the matters that involve us and the saints. We should consider the source of a matter and its consequences before making decisions. We must learn this lesson. Every doctor must carefully consider the medication that should be given to a patient. We cannot be rash and careless or crude and coarse; rather, we must always be careful and cautious. We need to spend time before the Lord to carefully consider how to deal with others. Since we are building up the church, we must learn to discern matters. This applies to the administration of the church, the ministry of the word, and our contact with others.

HOW TO KNOW MATTERS

In our contact with people we must discern matters. Although we cannot interfere in the matters that do not involve us, we should not neglect the matters that involve us. Hence, we must learn to discern matters. However, our learning should be gradual, not in haste.

In learning to know matters, several points require our attention. First, behind every matter is a person. When the person is right, the matter is often right. For this reason, we should always know who is the source of a matter. We need to know the initiator, the sponsor, of the matter. If there is a problem with the source, there will be problems even if the matter appears right. We need to get to the bottom of every matter.

Second, we need to know the motive behind a matter. A person may donate ten thousand dollars to win the praise of others. Another person may give ten thousand dollars because others rebuked him for not giving. The motive is wrong in both situations. We should pay attention to people's motives. This does not mean that everything is right when the motive is right. We also need to know if the nature is right. For example, a brother who desires something improper may receive help from another brother. Although the helping brother may be motivated by love, the object of his help is something that is improper.

Third, even if the nature is right, we need to know if the way of carrying it out is right. For instance, a brother who wants to make an offering of ten thousand dollars may simply present the money to us. We should help him to understand that this is not the right way. He should put the money in the offering box. We should teach him to pray in order to know the needs in the church. Then he will see that his offering is not for one individual or for one purpose. We teach him by fellowshipping with him. When he goes to the Lord, the church will be built up. On the one hand, we should not simply think that an offering of ten thousand dollars is wonderful; on the other hand, we should not casually reject him. We must learn the best way to take care of this matter and be aware of the result.

Fourth, we must know what the result of a matter will be. The way something is carried out may be good, but the effect might not be good. If the effect is not good, the matter should not be touched. This is only a brief sketch. The administration of the church, the ministry of the word, and the visiting of the saints should be carried out according to these considerations. If we practice this, it will be easy for us to discern matters. When we discern matters in this way, we will build up rather than damage the church. Therefore, we must learn to know the source and nature of a matter so that we can find an appropriate way to handle it for the building up of the church.

If there is a problem with the offering one, we should help him with his person. If he has a wrong motive, we should help him. If there is a problem with the way it is carried out, its result, or its effect, we should neither ignore the problem nor handle it casually, because it impacts the building up of the church. We should help the brother with the appropriate adjustment, help, and teaching. This will build up the church.

If we handle matters carelessly or neglect them, we will miss the opportunity to build up the church. We should understand every matter that comes to us, and we should grasp the opportunity to edify and teach those who are involved. This will build up the church. If the saints can receive the help from us in the matter of material offering, they will be genuinely edified. They will also be built into the church.

In our work and service we must realize that being proud is meaningless and that considering ourselves inferior is even worse. There is no value in thinking that we are always right; neither is there any value in thinking that we are always wrong. Both are incorrect and worthless. Whenever we encounter a person or a matter, we should learn to know the strengths and weaknesses of the person as well as the source and nature of the matters. In this way we will know how to help a person be built up into the church; we will know also how to handle the matter. This is building.

BEING WATCHFUL AGAINST A SENSE OF NATIONAL SUPERIORITY AND WORLDLY CUSTOMS

The building up of the church does not depend on our acknowledgment of Western things as good. Even if eighty percent of the things from the West are good, at least twenty percent of the things in the East are also good. We should not think that people from the West are one hundred percent correct. Otherwise, the churches in the East and in the West will not be built up together.

Two days ago a Western brother said that several serving ones from the workers' house were at a birthday party with his family. He invited the serving ones from the workers' house to rejoice with them on his child's birthday. We should not bring worldly customs into our midst. In taking the way of the Lord's recovery, we have not celebrated birthdays for the past thirty years. We are not without fault, but some Western missionaries should be criticized. They have come to the East to do the Lord's work, but they are also damaging the Lord's work. To celebrate their children's birthday and even invite serving ones to participate is a fleshly act that will damage the Lord's work.

This may encourage those who live in the workers' house to celebrate their children's birthdays. This is intolerable. We have allowed the brothers from the West to influence us instead of our influencing them. Those who labor for the Lord must be very careful. Whenever we receive an invitation, we must know who is involved and the purpose of the gathering. We preach the truth concerning not loving the world, and we desire that others would not love the world. For the past thirty years the co-workers have not celebrated birthdays for our children or even our parents. We must learn this lesson to build up the church. Otherwise, our labor will be according to a Chinese proverb which says that we are grinding soybeans without producing any tofu. Our labor will be in vain. For this reason, we must not be proud or overly humble in knowing the source of a matter.

Before inviting a Western brother to speak, we considered the fact that he had publicly thanked those who sent him Christmas cards. Although I received spiritual help from this brother, in this matter he needed to be helped. If Christmas is condemned by God, then even if people send us cards, we should not thank them. This example shows that not all things from the West are right. They need our help in many matters. Although they have no light concerning the church ground, they refuse to be helped in this matter. They even debate and argue repeatedly concerning the church ground. This displays a sense of national superiority. In order for the churches in the East and the West to be built up, the brothers from the West must be open to the church ground. We have not been playing games for the past thirty years. We have given our lives to take this way. We should not lightly consider any matter in the church. We should be desperate in some matters and let other matters go. We respect the spiritual ministries from the West, but we do not agree that everything from the West is correct.

The churches are before us. We accept the Western brothers who are with us, and we must allow them to serve the Lord. However, we must learn to know people and to discern matters. We must also know what we can and cannot accept. We even need to discern matters concerning a young brother or a young sister. We should encourage what is proper and restrict what is not proper. Merely preaching the gospel to save sinners and edifying the believers cannot build up the genuine church of the Lord. We must draw others to Christ and help them to be established and built up in the church.

CHAPTER NINE

THE MEANING OF BUILDING BEING IN THE BUILDING OF GOD'S AUTHORITY OVER MAN

Most people think that building enables us to coordinate together so that we are no longer separate individuals but a corporate Body. The real meaning of building, however, is to build Christ into the believers. When Christ has been built into the believers, they become His Body. In Ephesians 4:11-12 Paul says that God gave various gifts to the church for the building up of the Body of Christ, the building up of the church. In 1 Corinthians 3 he refers to the building up of the Body as the building of God's habitation. The Body and the habitation are the same thing. Paul tells us to use gold, silver, and precious stones for the building. If we build with wood, grass, and stubble, our work will be consumed (vv. 12-15).

Verse 12 of chapter 3 shows that the building materials are gold, silver, and precious stones. Gold signifies the divine nature of God the Father; silver signifies the redemption of Christ, the Son; and precious stones signify the transforming work of the Spirit. This shows that the material for the building is the Triune God—the Father, the Son, and the Spirit. In other words, the building is built with the Father's divine nature, the Son's redemption, and the Spirit's transforming work. This verse, however, does not say what we are building. For example, brick, stone, or wood refer to the materials for building, but a home, a classroom, or an auditorium refers to the actual building.

According to the Bible, there are two aspects to God's building in the universe: one is a dwelling place, and the other is a city. Everything concerning the building is related either to the dwelling place or to the city. Whether God or man is building, there are only two aspects to the building—the dwelling place and the city. *Dwelling place, temple,* and *palace* refer to the same thing. A temple is a dwelling place, and a palace is a dwelling place. With the exception of the tower of Babel, every building spoken of in the Bible is either a dwelling place or a city. Today God is building a dwelling place. The church is God's dwelling place, God's house. When this building is accomplished, it will be a city—the New Jerusalem. According to Ephesians 2:22, God is building a dwelling place; according to Hebrews 11:10, God is building a city with foundations.

THE BUILDING OF GOD'S TEMPLE

In the Old Testament the holy temple typifies God's dwelling place, and the holy city typifies the New Jerusalem. When the children of Israel entered into Canaan, from their point of view they obtained the blessing of a land flowing with milk and honey. From God's point of view, however, they were building a temple and a city for God (1 Kings 8:12-21). The Israelites took the holy temple and the holy city, Jerusalem, as their center. When the children of Israel arrived in Canaan, their work was to build the temple and the city. All of God's dealings with His people in the Old Testament were related to the temple and the city. Hence, the psalmists often spoke of the holy temple and the holy city. This is the central matter between God and His people.

Satan, God's enemy, did everything he could to damage the relationship between God and His people. Satan did this by destroying the holy temple and the holy city. After the destruction of the temple and the holy city, there was a recovery among the people of Israel. The building needed to be recovered. The holy temple and the holy city needed to be built. This shows that the building up of the Body of Christ is the building up of God's temple on the one hand and the building up of God's city on the other. On one hand, the Body of Christ is God's house, God's dwelling place, and God's temple; on the other hand, the Body of Christ is the church and the bride of Christ. In Revelation 21 we see a city—the

New Jerusalem. This holy city is the bride. Therefore, the church is a matter of the temple and the city. To build up the church is to build up God's temple and God's city.

THE BUILDING OF THE TEMPLE BEING THE BUILDING OF THE MINGLING OF GOD AND MAN

To build the church, the Body of Christ, is a general expression in the Bible. A more specific and definite expression is to build up the temple and the city. The emphasis of the temple is on God's presence, the mingling of God and man. Hence, to build up the temple is to build up the mingling of God and man. First Corinthians 6:19 says, "Do you not know that your body is a temple of the Holy Spirit within you?" We are God's temple, and God's Spirit dwells within us. This is the mingling of God and man. The temple is a matter of God mingling with man. After the temple was built, the glory of Jehovah filled the whole temple (1 Kings 8:10-11). This temple signifies the children of Israel becoming God's dwelling place; God dwelt among them. In the administration of the church and the ministry of the word we are building up the church. We are building the mingling of God and man into people. The purpose of the administration of the church is to produce the mingling of God and man. The purpose of our ministering the word is also to produce the mingling of God and man. If we produce the mingling of God and man, we are building up the temple.

This principle can be applied to many situations. There may be two brothers who live together but cannot get along. They do not quarrel and are polite, but there is no building. I may ask, "Is God's presence with them? Is God's temple there?" If there is no building between them, they do not have God's presence or the temple. They are independent persons, neither of whom cares for the affairs of the other. They are simply two brothers who serve the Lord together and who live in the same house. They do not have God's presence, His temple.

If we have been built and have learned the lesson of building, we will realize that these brothers are lacking in the mingling. They both have a substantial amount of the self, and therefore there is not much mingling with the Lord. Hence, our work is to build them up so that Christ can be mingled more with them. We need to pay special attention to the parts of their being that do not allow them to be mingled with God. If they would allow those parts to be dealt with, they would be mingled with God, and God's temple would be in them. The extent of our being joined to others depends on how much we have been mingled with God. This is the building, and it is God's temple with His presence.

Whenever we truly render spiritual help to people, we enable them to be mingled more with God. The more they are mingled with God, the more they will be joined to the other members of the Body. Those who are short of the element of God cannot be one with other believers. Therefore, the brothers who speak from the podium must be sure that their words will issue in God being mingled more with the saints. If we work with young people, the messages we speak should cause them to be mingled more with God. If our messages do not have this result, our work is not a building work. We are not building the temple. A work that builds the temple is a work that allows God to obtain a dwelling place. It allows God to dwell in man. Our work must cause God to dwell more in man and to be mingled with man.

THE BUILDING OF GOD'S CITY

There is a distinction between the temple and the city. The temple emphasizes a dwelling place, a habitation. The city is a matter of administration. Therefore, the temple is a matter of presence, and the city is a matter of sovereign power, authority. When the New Jerusalem appears, these two matters will be combined. The New Jerusalem is a city, which is a matter of authority, and God's tabernacle with men, which is a matter of dwelling. Hence, in the New Jerusalem we see both God's presence and God's authority. Although both aspects are combined, the emphasis in the city is on authority. Hence, the center of the New Jerusalem is the throne of God and of the Lamb, which is a matter of God's sovereign power, God's authority (Rev. 22:3).

THE BUILDING OF THE CITY BEING THE BUILDING OF GOD'S AUTHORITY OVER MAN

To build the temple is to build God's habitation that God may have the ground in man, dwell in man, and mingle Himself with man. To build the city is to build God's sovereign power, God's authority, over man. We first must build God's presence into man. This is the initial step. Then we need to build God's sovereign power, His authority, over man. This is the final step. Therefore, first there is the church, the house of God, the temple of God, and then there is the manifestation of the New Jerusalem. In the building work we always build the temple first and then the city. God's presence comes before God's authority. First, we build God's mingling within man, and then we build God's authority over man.

Although the temple is the center, the protection is with the city. A person who has only the element of the temple, not the city, has no protection. If there is only a recovery of the temple, without a city, then the temple will have no protection. For this reason, after the temple was recovered with Ezra, Nehemiah still needed to recover the city. There was no battle during the recovery of the temple, because the matter of protection was not at issue; however, there was a threat of war when the city was being recovered because the city was related to protection.

God's presence does not imply warfare, but God's authority is related to warfare. Satan's work in people is to destroy God's authority, not God's presence. The ultimate purpose of God is His authority, not His presence. The ultimate manifestation in the Bible is a city with the throne of God at its center. This means that God's ultimate goal is to work out something in which He can reign and establish His throne.

When we are mingled with God and have His presence, we can be joined with others as God's temple. Those who are mingled with God and have His presence can be joined together to become God's temple. However, this does not make us God's city. We must be built to the extent that we are under God's authority, that we have God's sovereign power over us. Only then can we be joined together to become a city. If we only have God's mingling, God can only have a dwelling place. In order for God to reign among us, we must have God's authority over us.

Hence, the meaning of building is to build God's presence into people and to build God's reign over them, that is, to build God's mingling into people and to build God's ruling over them. If there is no temple or city on earth, God is restricted to heaven and can reign only in heaven. Only when there is a temple on earth can God dwell on earth, and only when there is a city on earth can God's will be done on earth and His reign be exercised on earth. In other words, when we have been inwardly built by God and thus have His presence, we will be joined with those who have also been built by God and thus have His presence to become His temple. Then when we have God's authority and reigning over us, we can be joined with those who are also under God's authority to become a city.

For this reason, we must allow God to work in us so that we may be built. If there is a matter in which we are not mingled with God, we are not His temple. If we do not allow God to reign in us in a matter, we are not God's city. We must let God build in us. After we are built, we will know whether the inward being of a person whom we contact is desolate or whether he has God's presence. We will know also whether he has been built and has God's temple in him. Perhaps he zealously loves the Lord, but we touch only desolation in him. He does not have God's presence when he deals with different things. At best, we can sense that he is zealous, active, and resolute, but we cannot see the temple in him. We cannot touch God's presence in him. Therefore, he cannot serve in coordination with other Christians.

In order to help such a person, we need to do the work of building to build God into him. In other words, we need to build God's presence into him so that he can have a measure of God's temple, God's presence, and God's mingling. In this small measure of God's presence and mingling, we are also built into him. With this small measure of God's presence and mingling, he can be joined with us. With this small measure of God's presence and mingling, he is built, not isolated. The more we work on this person, the more God's presence and mingling within him will increase, God's temple in him will increase, and his joining with others will increase in measure. The more he is built in this way, the more he will be saved from being independent. The more he is built in this way, the more he will be saved from being individualistic and the more he will learn to be joined with others to be built together.

After we have worked on a person for some time, he will have some building in him, and he will eventually have God's temple in him. However, he still does not have God's city. He still does not know God's authority, God's sovereign power. The city is altogether a matter of authority. When the city and the tower of Babel were built on earth, man overthrew God's authority (Gen. 11:3-4). When we build God's temple into a person, we must also build God's city—God's sovereign power, His authority—into him. Then he will learn not only to have God's presence but also to be under God's authority in everything.

What does it mean to be under God's authority? What is authority? Not only must we see that there is authority and order in the church, but we must also see that the entire universe is a matter of authority. For example, when Michael the archangel contended with the devil concerning the body of Moses, he did not dare to bring a reviling judgment against the devil. He only said, "The Lord rebuke you" (Jude 9). This is a matter of authority. In Matthew 8 the centurion said to the Lord, "I also am a man under authority, having soldiers under me. And I say to this one, Go, and he goes; and to another, Come, and he comes" (v. 9). This is a matter of authority. The entire universe is a matter of authority, a matter of order. There is order in our homes. Order involves authority. This applies even more so to the church.

Since the beginning of Genesis, the universe has been in chaos because order was lost. In the New Testament, beginning with the Gospel of Matthew, God has been doing a work of recovery. As He accomplishes the work of recovery, there is more order. By the end of Revelation everything is in proper order. Therefore, when the city is manifested, everything will be under authority. The building work we are doing begins with building God's mingling into man and consummates with the building of God's authority over man. The more a person is mingled with God and the more authority of God a person has, the more he will be joined with others. Merely having good conduct is not enough in the church, because the church is a matter of being built under God's authority.

THE TEMPLE AND THE CITY BEING EQUALLY CRUCIAL

Our work is to let people know what it means to have the mingling of God and man and what it means to be under God's authority. Without the mingling and without God's authority, there can be no building. Without the temple, there is no dwelling place; without the city, there is no protection. In other words, if we know God's presence without knowing His authority, we do not have the city and the temple. God's presence will eventually be lost because there is no protection. We must have God's presence as well as His authority in order to have protection.

The building always involves warfare. Ephesians 2 speaks of building, and chapter 6 speaks of spiritual warfare. Warfare is related to the city, not the temple; warfare is for God's authority, not His presence. When Nehemiah returned to build the city, he encountered warfare (Neh. 4:7-8). It seems as if the enemy did not desire to frustrate the building of the temple as much as he desired to frustrate the building of the city. This is because the city involves God's authority. The enemy is clear that if there is no city, the temple can easily be destroyed; hence, he damages the matter of authority and order. If there is no city, the temple has no protection. Satan knows that God's presence can be easily destroyed when there is no order, no authority, in the church.

Every worker of the Lord needs to understand the meaning of building the church. To build the church is to build up God's authority in the church. If a local church has only zeal, warmth, and mutual love but no order or authority, that church is wrong. That church has no protection. Although such a church may be very good today, the lack of protection may cause it to collapse tomorrow.

Loving one another does not necessarily mean God's presence; it may be something of the natural human emotions and not have the mingling of God. Even if we have the mingling of God, if we do not possess His authority, there is no protection. Authority must be established in the church. A church is very weak if the brothers speak differently when a situation arises. Instead of there being building in that church, there is a pile of stones. A strong church is full of God's presence and God's authority, having the temple as well as the city.

It is difficult to find God's authority in Christianity. Most groups are full of human opinions. They dignify themselves by saying that they are being democratic. However, they are full of human opinions and lack God's authority. This was the condition of the church in Laodicea. This is the reason deacons argue with elders, and elders argue with pastors. Our intention is not to criticize others but to unveil the fact that if we disregard God's authority and emphasize man's opinion, the result is endless quarrelling.

The church of God is a temple and a city. In the church of God there are the temple and the city—God's presence and His authority. We must consider the type of work we are doing. Are we building the church or Christianity? We must first know whether we are under God's authority and are keeping our position in the order arranged by God. Few people realize that to build the church is to build God's presence and authority. From this time onward, however, we must see that to build up the Body of Christ is to build up the mingling of God and man and to build up God's authority over man. We must do this work.

ALLOWING GOD TO BE BUILT INTO US

Our being built into God means that we allow God to work in us and to mingle Himself with us in everything. If we are built by God and are subjected under His authority, we can then help others by doing a work of building in them. When we work on others, we first add God into them so that they have God's presence in their practical walk and living. In this way they become God's temple. We must then do another work in them so that they know God's authority. This is to build up the wall in them. In this way they will have God's presence and authority. They are built-up persons no matter where they go. They know what it is to have God's presence, God's mingling; they also know God's authority and God's order. They have been built.

Some brothers and sisters may be zealous, but they do not have God's temple or God's city. They may have a certain amount of God's presence, but they do not understand God's authority. There is a measure of the recovery of Ezra but nothing of the recovery of Nehemiah. However, others have both the temple and the city. They have God's presence and God's authority. In everything they have God's mingling, and they are under God's authority. They keep the order and are under authority. They are also reigning, because they have God's authority. In other words, they have God's city. When we have God's city within us, we have protection for our spiritual condition.

KNOWING THE STRATAGEMS OF THE ENEMY

The Old Testament says that the city of David was David's stronghold (1 Chron. 11:5, 7). Therefore, when Nehemiah went forth to recover the city, the enemies appeared (Neh. 4:7-8), and those who built the wall did the work with one hand and held a weapon with the other (v. 17). This type is clear. It means that those who build the church must build and fight at the same time. Authority is a protection to the church. We must fight for this authority. In order to fight for the authority of the church, we must learn the lesson. When we lead the brothers and sisters to love the Lord and live for Him, thereby enabling them to obtain God's presence, we will not encounter much warfare. However, as we lead the church to have a proper order and enter into God's authority, the enemy will come.

The book of Nehemiah shows that the first stratagem of the enemy is not a frontal assault. He attacks from the side. Those involved in the building work need to learn to fight in spiritual warfare. We first need to know how to deal with the enemy's stratagems. Paul says that we need to stand against the stratagems of the devil (Eph. 6:11). We are not ignorant of his schemes. Whenever we build up the order in the church, Satan will use skillful ways to destroy our work. He will make

THE MEANING OF BUILDING   115

a good proposal through a dear brother or sister. If we accept such a proposal, the entire building will be destroyed. The enemy's stratagems are often seen in the church. He is doing an exceedingly treacherous work. He is doing a work to damage the order in the church, to tear down the wall of the city. In spiritual warfare it is more crucial to understand the enemy's stratagems than it is to pick up a sword to deal with the enemy. This is what Nehemiah did. Nehemiah first understood the stratagems of the enemy. When the enemies said, "Come,...and let us take counsel together," Nehemiah's reply was, "None of these things that you are saying have happened; rather you have invented them in your own heart" (Neh. 6:1-9). Nehemiah saw through the enemies' stratagems. Therefore, in the building work we need to know persons, matters, and the schemes of the enemy. Our knowing the schemes of the enemy depends on our knowing persons and matters. If we do not know persons and matters, the enemy can hide in them. If Nehemiah had accepted the enemies' suggestions, he would have fallen victim to the enemies' stratagems. If we do not know a matter, we will not know the enemy's stratagems, and it will be easy for us to fall victim to his devices. The enemy desires to destroy God's authority, the order, in the church.

For example, there was once the problem of whether the cup for the Lord's table should be a large cup or small individual cups. This problem is actually a matter of authority, not of the size of the cup. In principle, the elders in our district or local church should have the administrative authority to determine what size the cup should be. The administrative authority for this problem is with the elders, not the ones responsible for a group meeting. This is not a small matter. It is a very important principle. If we would build up and administrate the church, the determination of the size of the cup is not related to the truth but to the elders' decision. We should obey the representative authority of the elders.

Even if a local church uses a large cup, but a district wants to use small cups, the decision still depends on the elders. It is an administrative matter. There is no need for discussions related to the size of the cup for the table meeting and what to use for the baptistery apart from the elders; such discussions can only cause chaos and lawlessness. This indicates a lack of knowing authority. In other words, there is no building in the matter of authority.

Strictly speaking, we may express our opinion any place other than the church. If we want to take the way of the Gentiles to practice democracy in the church, we will lose God's presence and protection. We must know God's building work, and we must know God's presence and authority. In matters relating to the church, those who serve the Lord should not talk freely. Expressing our opinions makes the church a debate club.

This does not mean that we should not express our considerations; rather, it means that we should see the authority of God. A brother responsible for a group meeting should deal with problems according to the proper channel. He can fellowship with the elders and let them know his feeling. The problem should be brought to the elders. The elders should not hastily reject the feeling of the brother. Rather, they should bring the brother's feeling to the Lord and see how the Lord will lead them. This is proper. The responsible brother should then follow the decision of the elders without any opinion. The elders may feel to follow the feeling of the brother. They may also feel that the whole church should take the same way. This is a proper church.

BUILDING UP THE PROPER AUTHORITY IN THE CHURCH

The church should function in this way, and the administration of any country should also function in this way. New measures are not produced by quarrels. In order for a new measure to become a law, the legislative body of a country must function appropriately and legally. Quarrels are not effective. We must learn this lesson. When a problem is before us, we should not express numerous different opinions. There is no need to quarrel in the church. Rather, we should build up the authority, the wall, to protect all the saints in the church. We must learn this lesson in order to do a serious work. Satan's stratagem is to damage God's building. For this reason, we should not encourage the atmosphere of freely expressing our opinions. Such an atmosphere will damage the church. We should not encourage fleshly activities or the expression of human opinions in the church. We should receive the dealing from the Lord and allow the Lord to build Himself into us.

The ones who have learned the lesson before the Lord and have been perfected know that there is order in the church. This does not mean that such ones are an authority; rather, they keep their position. If we have not learned the lesson and have not been built by God, our work will not be for the building. Those who are saved through us will be wild because we have not been built by God. Those whom we perfect will also be wild. We will not be able to build because we have not passed through the process of being built. Consequently, the Lord will have no way in us.

Today Christianity is chaotic. There are many opportunities for those who take the way of chaos. They can even establish a congregation at will. But those who desire to do the work of God's building need to learn serious lessons and see through the enemy's stratagems. This does not involve the truth. Our opinion may be correct, but we can still be persons who do not walk according to order, do not obey authority, and have not been dealt with. Because we have not learned the lesson, we will not know the church.

A brother responsible for a group meeting does not have the authority to decide something concerning the administration of the church. If the churches in Taiwan use large cups for the Lord's table, it is foolishness for a group meeting to change to small cups. This proves that we have not learned any lessons and do not know the church and the building. This shows that we are presumptuous and audacious persons. We must learn this serious lesson, and then we can do a serious work. Such a work will be valuable because it will be the building.

Building up authority does not mean building up our personal authority; rather, it means building up God's order in the church. When a person touches this authority, he will realize that this is the church and that God's order is here. God can have a way, and we will have a way. For hundreds of years many people have taken the way of Christianity. However, that is not God's way. May the Lord be gracious to us that we would know His building for the administration of the church and for the ministry of the word.

CHAPTER TEN

SELECTING MATERIAL
FOR THE MINISTRY OF THE WORD

THE MINISTRY OF THE WORD BEING
FOR PEOPLE TO RECEIVE THE LIFE SUPPLY

A minister of the word must pay attention to the material he uses. The selection of material is an important matter and involves many details. Those who minister the word need to understand that the ministry of the word is for the life supply. Our ministering the word also should solve people's problems and generate a feeling of need in them. It should not merely give them things to consider. Our ministering the word must supply people with life, solve their problems, and create a feeling of need in them. We must follow these principles when we select material for the ministry of the word.

More books have been produced on the subject of Christianity than on any other subject. The number of books on biblical exposition is especially large. If a minister of the word thinks that he does not need to use material from others' publications, he is proud and foolish. A minister of the word may also be tempted to believe that he only needs material from books published in Christianity. Such a minister has lost the ministry of the word. A minister of the word should not depend only on material found in books.

THE BASIC MATERIAL
FOR THE MINISTRY OF THE WORD
BEING LESSONS LEARNED PERSONALLY
AND BURDENS RECEIVED FROM THE LORD

The basic material for the ministry of the word should be the lessons a person has learned and the burdens he has received from the Lord. We may want to release a message based upon a lesson we learned and a burden we received. We may consult others for their views, explanations, and illustrations related to the lesson we learned and the burden we received. It is helpful to read reference books regularly to broaden our knowledge, but if a minister of the word compiles his messages from reference books without learning any lessons or receiving any burdens, his speaking is degraded and useless. The ministry of the word is based upon the lessons we have learned and the burdens we have received. If a minister of the word does not learn any lessons and never receives any burdens from the Lord, he should not speak from the podium.

For this reason, those who minister the word must continually learn lessons by being dealt with by the Lord in great and small things. He should also learn to receive burdens. He should receive a burden to preach the gospel and to give a message. He must continually receive burdens. Although the brothers and sisters fervently love the Lord, the building is lacking among us. Thus, there is the need for us to receive the burden to lead the brothers and sisters into the feeling that they need building. We should receive such a burden from the Lord and release this burden through the ministry of the word.

NOT BEING PROUD BUT WATCHING OVER OUR HEART

In the ministry of the word we should not be proud. It is foolish to be proud as we prepare, thinking that our material is better than anyone else's. Even if our material is better, when we consult with others, our knowledge will be broadened and our feeling for the word will be deepened. Hence, as we select material for the ministry of the word, on the one hand, we should check and see if the lessons we have learned and the burden we have received are our basis, and on the other hand, we should watch over our heart so that we are not proud.

A person's speaking is degraded and sinful if he must search for material from books because he has nothing to speak. The release of the word that is not based on experience or a burden received from the Lord is an offense to God. Such a careless speaking is sin. Every message must be based on personal experience and released from a burden. This is the fundamental basis for the release of the word. When we release the word, we should not be proud. We should be open to using reference books and receiving help from others. For example, if we read a book several years ago on a particular topic, it will do no harm to read it again. Our heart and attitude at this point are to consult other material and to receive help from others. However, we should not collect material indiscriminately. This is the right attitude and the right heart.

SELECTING MATERIAL THAT IS LIVING, NOT NEW AND UNUSUAL

In our preparation to minister the word, we must look for material that is living, not dead. If those who minister the word desire to be different from others, they will be tempted to select material that is new and unusual but also dead. Thus, their messages are frivolous and do not have the taste of life. Hence, when we prepare a message, we should avoid the thought of being original by using material that is new and unusual. Instead, we should endeavor to give messages that are living and full of life supply. For example, though others have spoken concerning regeneration many times, we should still speak of it. Regeneration is an old topic that does not have anything new or unusual, but if our material is living, our speaking will be full of supply and taste. If we only care to tell stories and neglect the supply of life, we are simply professional storytellers. Although the saints may laugh, our speaking will be an offense to the Lord.

AVOIDING THE EXPOUNDING OF SCRIPTURE

When looking for material, we should avoid expounding Scripture. The Bible is not a simple book. If we speak from the Bible, we will not have many problems, but if we expound the Bible, we will have many problems, because speaking from the Bible is different from expounding the Bible. We can release a message based on a few verses. For example, when we quote Hebrews 2:3, "How shall we escape if we have neglected so great a salvation," to stir up people's appreciation of salvation, we are speaking from the Bible. But when we try to explain the meaning of the words *salvation* and *neglect*, we are expounding the Bible. Those who speak from the podium must avoid expounding Scripture. They can speak from the Bible, but they should not expound it.

Expounding the Bible is a serious matter. Hence, we should avoid material that expounds Scripture since such material does not contain much life and is subject to error. Strictly speaking, only those with the gift of teaching should expound Scripture, and not everyone has this gift. The words in the Bible can be used to speak a message, but expounding the Bible can cause problems. Hence, it is best to avoid books that expound the Bible.

Most of the books that expound the Bible impart knowledge to people but do not supply much life. In addition, there are many ways to expound the Bible. The same portion of the Word often has many different interpretations. When I was young, I read a good book concerning the seventy weeks in the book of Daniel. After reading the book, I began to speak what I had learned to others. I later realized that I was behaving like a fool, and I laughed at myself because there are many interpretations of the seventy weeks, and each interpretation seems logical. It is a serious matter to expound the Bible. We should try our best to avoid expounding the Bible.

Throughout the centuries most sermons were based on Bible verses. For example, Dr. John Sung used the "flow of blood" in Luke 8:43 to give a sermon on the Lord's precious blood, without expounding the verse. We should avoid expounding the Bible unless we are establishing a biblical basis. Exposition is to meet a need for establishing a biblical basis. We should expound the Bible within the boundary of this real basis. We should stay within this boundary; otherwise, our message will be dead. We must hold on to the basic principle that the message must be living. If we want our message to be living, we cannot speak empty doctrine; we must not merely expound the Bible.

We should expound the Bible only when we need a biblical basis to convey a thought to people. As long as such a need is met, there is no need for much explanation. Furthermore,

SELECTING MATERIAL FOR THE MINISTRY   123

quoting others may cause confusion among the saints because of the different viewpoints in the expositions.

The first time I read the Bible, I spent much time reading reference books concerning the prophecies in the Bible. In Matthew 24 the Lord Jesus said that "two women will be grinding at the mill; one is taken and one is left" (v. 41). An authoritative expositor among the Brethren said that the one who was left was the best, and he gave many reasons in support. How can the better one be left? We believe that the one who was taken was better. Therefore, if we do not have discernment, we will be misled.

There are many books in Christianity, so the ministers of the word are often tempted to use them. Although they need to consult different books, some of these books are inaccurate. For example, Andrew Murray truly knew the Lord inwardly, but his expositions were not always accurate. We can rely on his spiritual experiences, but we cannot always rely on him in Bible expositions.

When Brother T. Austin-Sparks was in Taiwan, he said that the New Jerusalem did not exist. He went beyond his portion and began to expound the Bible. We cannot accept this exposition. Even though we highly regard the spiritual matters Brother Austin-Sparks ministered to us, we cannot go along with this exposition. If there is no New Jerusalem, where will the believers be? For this reason we have been very careful in the matter of exposition. Generally speaking, it is not difficult to select material for the ministry of the word. But if we are not absolutely sure concerning material that expounds the Bible, we should not accept it. We also should not attempt to expound the Scripture unless it is absolutely necessary.

Throughout the centuries different spiritual persons have expounded the Bible, but it was difficult for them not to make mistakes. Andrew Murray, Brother Austin-Sparks, and even Mrs. Jessie Penn-Lewis made serious mistakes in exposition. Those of the inner life had good spiritual experiences but were far off in expounding Scriptures. Sister Dora Yu was very spiritual, but she also was inaccurate in expounding the Bible. She said that being saved was not equivalent to being regenerated, and those who were saved still needed to repent in order to be regenerated. Hence, we need to avoid Bible exposition when we select material. It is best not to select material that touches Bible exposition unless there is a definite need, and we are sure of its accuracy.

NOT CONVERTING THE MESSAGES INTO TEACHING MATERIAL

The basis and principle for selecting material are to supply people with life, to solve their problems, and to generate a feeling of need within them. This is how material should be selected for the young people's meeting. Although our messages may be educational, we should avoid turning them into a course of instruction. For example, the so-called Sunday school has become a course for fifty-two topics of study. A child may participate in all these lessons without gaining much inwardly related to spirituality, the content of the gospel, and the experience of life.

For example, I attended a Christian elementary school and was one of the top students in Sunday school. I even served as a teacher's assistant in Sunday school. But I did not gain anything from the Sunday school. For this reason, I said that we should drop the word *school* from the children's meetings. We do not want a Sunday school; we simply want children's meetings. We should not give children the concept that the children's meeting is a course of study, and that they are required to recite and memorize. They should feel that they are touched and inwardly supplied when they come. Hence, our children's meetings should focus on making these children godly young people who live before the Lord. If they can be impressed with matters concerning how to be a proper human being, fearing God, or salvation, it will be a help to them.

In a children's meeting in Manila, the serving ones wanted to tell the story of Samson and Delilah because several movie houses in Manila were showing the love story of Samson and Delilah. This is a basic mistake in selecting material. This way is wrong. We should not randomly speak to children about Samuel today, David tomorrow, Saul the following day, and then Peter, giving them outlines to memorize and then testing them on the material. This is futile, and it is wrong. We need to touch their feeling.

For example, the children's meetings that D. L. Moody conducted looked like Sunday school but were not. Moody was burdened for people's souls. One time he invited a little girl to attend his Sunday school. The girl promised to come but did not show up. Several days later Moody saw her on the street. As soon as she saw Moody, the girl ran into a tavern and hid under a bed. Moody ran after her and pulled her out from under the bed. After this, the little girl attended his Sunday school. If we are as burdened as Moody, we will succeed. We need to pay attention to this matter; all the other things are secondary.

We should not give lessons like elementary school teachers, who divide the children into groups and conduct classes. We should not give lessons to children and begin the class by asking, "What was the lesson last week? Right; it was on David. Who is David?" The children reply, "David was a person who is after God's heart." "David was a king for forty years." We then say, "Very good, you get one hundred percent." If our children's meetings are like this, we are doing a work of death, which should be stopped. The children's meeting in Taipei still has this flavor.

The material we use should be living. We might speak to the children about loving their brothers and sisters, about God's love, and how God created men with a loving heart. We do not need to speak about spiritual love. We should give them the feeling that the love within them comes from God and that they should love their brothers and sisters. They would then feel guilty if they do not love their brothers and sisters. In the next meeting we can speak about honoring our parents, asking them to obey their parents. This speaking is living. This does not mean that we should not use Bible stories. We can use a story in the Bible to illustrate loving our brothers and sisters. It is not a course of study, but a living application.

This should also be applied to the work with the young brothers and sisters. Those who serve the young saints must understand that we should not depend on edifying meetings. If we depend on edifying meetings, we will fail. From 1946 to 1948 there were no young people's meetings in Shanghai. We did not even have such a term. At the time the care for young people was from a burden. The saints shepherded them individually. It is a pity that our college conferences are conducted like classes teaching a subject. All of those who speak for the Lord must learn that our speaking should edify without being like a class. We are not conducting classes. This is dead, and it will not enliven people.

Those who speak must receive a burden to labor on the young people one by one. Through prayer and other ways we should shepherd them so that the Lord can gain them. We should not always teach them what Adam, Abel, Enoch, and Abraham did. They may memorize all this one week and forget it the next week. Teaching them in this way is futile. We should touch their feeling in a way that they will never forget. Mental exercise and recitation are but dead letters. There is no need to pay much attention to such things. Furthermore, we should not be concerned about how many are in attendance. Instead, we should endeavor to learn some living lessons, have living experiences, and receive a living burden to labor on the young brothers and sisters. We should do a work of kindling the fire in them that would cause them to kindle the fire in others. Only this kind of work is a living work.

LEARNING TO TOUCH OTHERS DEEP WITHIN

In the same principle, when we give a message, we should avoid speaking in a scientific way. For example, we have failed if we teach people only according to the main headings and subheadings of an outline. Even though it is not bad to read an outline, it is more important to learn to touch people's feeling. If we overemphasize memorizing an outline, the saints might not be able to remember the points. Even if they are able to remember the points, they will forget them if they have not touched something. The brothers who minister may speak much, but their first priority must be to give people something living and to touch their inner being. In this way, even if people forget the outline, something solid will still remain in them.

Furthermore, we should learn not to bring the training into the meetings. Trainings are different in nature from church meetings. We must not treat the brothers and sisters like trainees. The brothers and sisters may forget the outline and Scripture verses, but if they are touched by something, after the meeting they will pray, confess their sins, and even preach the gospel. If this is the case, the speaking is living and supplying. The meat of a steak is attached to the bones, but when we serve the steak, we should give meat instead of bones. An outline is important because many points on the outline can touch people's feeling. However, when we feed people, we should give them "meat" instead of "bones," because few people can chew bones. This is a great matter.

Hence, we should learn to use material that can touch people's feeling so that they are touched even if they do not understand much of the message. Such speaking is powerful because it is clear and rich in content without stressing logical reasoning skills. Rather, it touches the feeling deep within people.

We have a heavy burden concerning our ministry of the word. The ministry of the word is very weak on the Lord's Day morning, in the midweek meeting, in the home meetings, in the young people's meeting, and even in the children's meeting. There are problems with the ministry of the word. The speaking is too weak, resulting in a weakened situation among the saints. The main reason for the weak speaking is that it is dead. When the speaking is dead, the overall supply is weakened. Hence, all the brothers who bear the responsibility to minister the word must endeavor to look for a way for our speaking to render a living supply and not be dead. This requires that we no longer speak as if we are conducting a class with the rigid use of outlines. Our spiritual life requires teaching, but we cannot be rigid. We must avoid materials that resemble teaching materials in a school. We should not give the brothers and sisters homework; rather, we should touch their feeling to plant something solid into them.

If we fail to do this in our ministry of the word, we do not have the ability to minister the word. If we have the ability to minister, we will touch the feeling of the saints and supply them with life whether we stutter or are eloquent, and whether the brothers and sisters like or dislike us.

THE CHURCH URGENTLY NEEDING
TO DO THE BUILDING WORK
THROUGH THE MINISTRY OF THE WORD

We have reached the critical point of urgently needing the building. If we merely save sinners and edify them, we are repeating the work of Christianity for the past one hundred years. This work has not resulted in the building or the dwelling place of God. When a person is built up in Kaohsiung, if he leaves Kaohsiung to go to either Hualien or Tainan, he is still built up. Even though he leaves Kaohsiung, he has not left the building; he is still a part of the spiritual house, which is not limited by time or space. Wherever he goes, he is built up in the Body of Christ. In God's unique building in the universe he is a built-up person. He is different from a person who is merely saved. He is different from a person who is spiritual. He is built up. Only such a person can be part of God's dwelling place and can function as a member of the Body of Christ wherever he goes.

God needs such a group of people on the earth today. He urgently needs a work of building. If we want to participate in this work, we need the administration of the church, and even more, we need the ministry of the word. The ministry of the word is first, and the administration of the church is second. Presently our greatest lack is in the ministry of the word. This is a serious problem. All our meetings are poor, weak, low, cold, dead, and shallow because we lack the ministry of the word. The administration of the church is second in importance. Therefore, the brothers who often speak on the podium must regard this matter seriously and endeavor to learn the lesson concerning ministering the word. We must never depend on our seniority. We should not think that because we have been speaking for many years, we can simply put together a message from our notes and reference books. Such a message will have no value or impact. It will not touch others, and it will not hit the mark.

We need to learn to always trouble the brothers and sisters when they listen to a message. They should be pricked even if they forget the subject and miss the content. They should feel as if they were stung by a mosquito. As a result they will be unable to rest after the meeting because something has been injected into their being.

The sisters should also have this skill when they visit others. Asking others whether they have read the Bible or prayed embarrasses people. We must not be dead; rather, we should learn to be living and learn some skills. We may not touch anything spiritual, but unknowingly a spiritual shot is injected. We may speak with people about the world they love, but by the end of our speaking they are "stung." They cannot rest and are troubled. We need to learn how to do this.

THE MINISTRY OF THE WORD AND THE SERVICE IN THE CHURCH NEEDING TO HAVE A LIVING COORDINATION

We must fellowship, through prayer and consideration, with those whom we serve concerning the content of our speaking. When I was serving in northern China, between 1940 and 1943, there was a brother whose situation was in my constant consideration. Sometimes I received a burden while I was speaking from the podium, and I would say that this brother needed to be visited. The brothers and sisters who heard this received a burden and visited him. Presently, however, because all the brothers endeavor to be unique in their speaking in order to become famous, they are not concerned about receiving a burden. This cannot be considered service.

It is regretful that the brothers in northern China did not leave the mainland. The messages they gave met the practical need and were not compiled hastily. When saints returned from visiting the brothers and sisters, they gave a report of their visit. On Monday mornings we would fellowship concerning the condition of the brothers and sisters from eight in the morning until three in the afternoon. Sometimes we would even fast and pray for them. As a result we learned many lessons. We studied how to help those who were having problems and how to deal with the problems. Often after a person was visited, he became living. Our speaking and our visitation worked together. But this working together was not by discussion; it was in spontaneity. This is true and practical coordination.

The speaking from the podium was living, and those who came to the meetings were also living. Many of the saints were amazed that what was released in the message met their exact need. Whenever they came to a meeting, their problem was solved. The speaking touched their problem and their inner being; hence, their problem was solved, and their need was met. What was spoken was the living word. This was the situation for almost two years, because the serving ones looked for a living word, rather than a routine speaking. They were not disorganized or loose, nor did they speak at will. Hence, wherever they went, their leading in the churches was living.

The best period of our coordination in the ministry of the word was between 1940 and 1943. Our present situation does not match the situation we had then. During that time the coordination between those serving and those ministering the word was living. Printing was not as convenient as it is today, and there were not that many arrangements, but everything was living.

CONCLUSION

In brief, we cannot be individualistic. We should learn to depend on others, relying on them for our life. We should learn to coordinate with others in service. We should not use dead ordinances or speak dead messages. Rather, we should study a living way and learn the lessons. Moreover, we should receive a burden and understand people's needs. We should know the different problems of the saints, the problems of the children, the young people, and the elderly ones. Based upon this knowledge, we can touch the elderly, the young people, and the parents when we speak. Everyone who hears the message will be touched. The church needs such a living word to bring in a living situation.

Today we encounter death in all our meetings. The children's meeting, the young people's meeting, and the Lord's Day meeting are all conducted according to dead ordinances. These meetings are our responsibilities. We cannot continue like this. The Lord's work and the church are suffering a great loss, and the main responsibility is with those who minister the word. The supply in the ministry of the word is important to the children, the young people, the parents, the elderly, and the working saints.

Chapter Eleven

THE IMPORTANCE AND THE COMMISSION OF THE MINISTRY OF THE WORD

CONCERNING THE BIBLE-READING MEETING

Some localities are doing well related to the administration of the church and the ministry of the word. Generally speaking, however, the administration of the church is weaker than the ministry of the word in all the localities. According to function, the ministry of the word is more important than the administration of the church. Hence, there is a greater need for the ministry of the word than for the administration of the church in all the localities.

The messages given on the Lord's Day are common and general. Since they are not living, they have become ordinary and routine and cannot produce any impact. Therefore, the churches should pay attention to the word ministered in all the meetings, not only on the Lord's Day. The word ministered in the other meetings often produces a definite impact. For instance, in one of the localities the Bible-reading meeting has been carried out successfully and is full of the Lord's presence.

Having a Person Responsible for the Meeting

Every local church should endeavor to give the brothers and sisters a heart to read the Bible so that they would love and enjoy reading the Bible. If possible, every locality should endeavor to have a meeting for the brothers and sisters to read the Bible. The Bible-reading meeting in the local church that we mentioned earlier has a person who is responsible for the meeting. On the one hand, the leading ones ask the saints to read the word; on the other hand, there is always a person responsible for the meeting, who is given at least twenty to thirty minutes to speak on some relevant matters. In their meetings the brothers and sisters share in the first half of the meeting, and then the person responsible develops the portion they read. This is a characteristic of their meeting.

Having the Spiritual Supply

Another characteristic is that in the development of the word by the brothers and sisters, the emphasis is not on logic or exposition but on the spiritual supply. Although the brothers and sisters study the Word, their development is not limited to simply reading the Word but to supplying life based on the spiritual light gleaned from a verse, a phrase, or the entire portion. There is a temptation in the Bible-reading meeting to require everyone to comprehend and memorize outlines. We should not fall into this temptation, because it will turn our meetings into a dead practice.

Our Bible-reading meetings, however, have somewhat fallen into this temptation. In helping the brothers and sisters to read the Word, we should not explain how different sections are divided, nor should we fellowship concerning the outline. Rather, we should share the light of life and the spiritual supply. A brother who has light and is strong in the Word should give a summary of twenty to thirty minutes. The first part of the meeting allows the Holy Spirit an opportunity to release the riches through the brothers and sisters and gives the brothers and sisters an opportunity to practice. But the Bible-reading meeting does not depend on this sharing. Whether the sharing from the brothers and sisters is rich or poor will not affect the meeting, because the speaking at the end supplies and feeds everyone.

If we depend only on the fellowship from the brothers and sisters, the meeting may not be strong and the saints' appetite for the meeting will be spoiled. They will not regard the Bible-reading meeting as important, and the attendance will drop. For example, in Taipei the number of participants in the Bible-reading meeting is gradually decreasing. One of the reasons may be the poor sharing. We should never make people feel that the Bible-reading meeting is insignificant. If people come to the meeting with an empty stomach and then go home with an empty stomach, they will feel that the meeting is a waste of their time. They will come with great anticipation and go home disappointed.

Furthermore, in the sharing and in the summary we must free ourselves from the outline. When the brothers and sisters begin reading the Bible, we can help them with the outline so that they may understand how the chapters are sectioned. But as the meetings continue, we should not focus on the outline; otherwise, our meeting can become dead.

Not Covering Much Material

In the Bible-reading meeting, it is best to read one chapter a week. It is not advisable to cover too much material. This can be compared to eating. If we swallow food without chewing, we cannot taste the food. One chapter a week may be considered rather slow. Since the saints come together only once a week, some churches encouraged the saints to read one chapter a day at home. In this way they can read six chapters in a week. This is very good. However, they should not cover all six chapters when they come together to fellowship. Instead, it is best to cover only one chapter. Hence, whether in giving a message or reading the Word together, we should never try to cover too much material. This is a great principle. It is very good to release one point in a meeting. Releasing two or more points may cause the meeting to lose its focus and be ruined. Therefore, it is not good to cover too much material.

If we read six chapters of the Bible per week, we will read more than three hundred chapters in fifty-two weeks, but we may not remember that much. However, if we read one chapter a week in the meeting with light and supply, we will read fifty-two chapters in a year. How rich that will be! This will give the saints a good impression and stir up their love for reading the Bible, causing them to read the Bible by themselves. They may even read six chapters a day. In this way they will build up the personal habit of reading the Bible.

Making the Word Tasty to People

Immediately after I was saved, I loved the Bible and was perfected in reading the Bible. We should extract the life supply from the Bible to feed the brothers and sisters. In this way they will acquire a taste, desire the supply, and enjoy reading the Bible. They will even enjoy reading the Bible by themselves.

If six chapters are covered in the Bible-reading meeting every week, there will not be any enjoyment, and the saints will become disinterested and bored. Therefore, we should not read too many chapters, lest our haste makes waste, and we get exactly the opposite effect. It is best to read one chapter, and extract the riches from this portion to feed the saints. Then the saints will feel that the Bible is so sweet and rich and will want to continue coming to the meeting. They will even study the Bible at home. Hence, it is not advisable to read many chapters in the Bible-reading meeting. However, the saints should read one or more chapters a day by themselves.

Those who are responsible for ministering the word must study how to conduct the Bible-reading meeting. We must first have some solid and nutritious food for the brothers and sisters. Then we must make the meeting "tasty" for the brothers and sisters. Of course, we should not use gimmicks, but we should give the saints the feeling that they have gained something. In this way they will even invite others to come and listen to the Lord's Word. Thus, the Bible-reading meeting and the ministry of the word are closely related.

Recently a church began a meeting for the pursuit of *Crucial Truths in the Holy Scriptures* on the Lord's Day evening. The number participating in this meeting was greater than that in the Lord's Day morning meeting. There were between one hundred forty to one hundred fifty people in the meeting even though the meeting hall can only accommodate approximately one hundred thirty people. Some people sat in the courtyard. Another church in the south of Taiwan began a Bible-reading meeting in which the attendance went from sixty people to one hundred forty. The saints gained a solid supply. It is worthwhile for us to study together.

The Supply of the Word
Having a Focus and Being General

When the brothers taking the lead in the Bible-reading

meeting sense that something is the need of the church, they should consider how to impress this point on the brothers and sisters. They should not speak concerning this point lightly but should repeat it emphatically until the saints receive it. In northern China I spent about five years speaking concerning the cross. Every day I hammered this burden into the saints. I used every opportunity to speak of the cross. My way was to repeatedly and continually drive the matter of the cross into every brother and sister. This practice is good but we should not carry it out too rigidly.

Furthermore, we should be general in emphasizing a burden so that other needs can be met. A local church should focus on the ministry of the word, but it should also take care of other aspects. For example, when I emphasized the cross in northern China, my speaking also covered other needs. We should observe everything and take care of matters as they arise. We need to take care of the elders, the deacons, those who visit people, and those who are burdened to preach the gospel. If we do not take care of all the needs, our locality may be perfected in one need but be lacking in another need. For example, if a brother continually speaks on the flesh, neglecting other needs, the bread-breaking meeting may become dry because everyone will be concerned with the flesh. Likewise, the gospel preaching will stop because everyone is speaking about the flesh. Even the church services may dry up. Therefore, we should take care of the various needs.

SUPPLYING THE WORD IN MEETINGS OF MUTUALITY

There is another need that we have not taken care of in the past. We should grasp the opportunity in every meeting of mutuality to supply others with the word. This can be in the prayer meeting, the bread-breaking meeting, and the fellowship meeting. In some localities there is no ministering of the word in the prayer meetings. Instead, the saints sing some hymns and pray a little. After this, the meeting is ended. Such a situation is neither normal nor proper.

Some of the brothers and sisters who come to a prayer meeting may be new believers, others might not know how to pray, and still others might not be in the mood to pray. Hence, without the ministry of the word, the meeting will be tasteless and the saints will lose the desire to attend the meeting. In other prayer meetings there is a lack in the ministry of the word and a lack in leading the saints to pray. The prayer meeting is like a boat without a rudder; it is tossed about in every direction by the wind. When the wind blows from the east, the meeting drifts toward the west; when the wind blows from the west, the meeting drifts toward the east. This kind of meeting is not attractive, and after filling up the time drifting here and there, the meeting will come to an end. This kind of meeting will not attract people; moreover, it is an offense to the Lord and to the brothers and sisters.

Therefore, in meetings such as the bread-breaking meeting, the prayer meeting, and the fellowship meeting, there should be a supply from the ministry of the word. The serving ones should not sleep peacefully; they should continually consider how to stir up the meetings. The meetings should be stirred up by the ministry of the word and by leading the saints in selecting hymns, praying, speaking, and giving announcements. The hearts of the brothers and sisters should be stirred up, and they should be helped to open their mouth one by one to pray in the meeting.

In particular, those who serve in the ministry of the word should release a word in every prayer meeting. But it should never be done in a rigid way. A word should also be released in the bread-breaking meeting, but it should not be done rigidly. We should be flexible. Something can be spoken before breaking the bread or after breaking the bread. One can even give a short word of fellowship while the bread and the cup are being passed. We should simply follow the flow of the Spirit. Those who minister the word should be prepared to release a word in the meetings.

Concerning the Bread-breaking Meeting

Many new believers do not have much knowledge concerning the significance of breaking the bread. Therefore, our continual speaking should stir them up in these matters. However, this kind of stirring up is not educational in nature. We can give an educational word in prayer meetings, but we should not do so in the bread-breaking meetings. These meetings differ in focus and in significance. There should not be anything educational in the bread-breaking meeting. An educational element will kill the meeting. If we feel the need for an educational word, it should be given after the bread is broken. Any word released before the bread is broken or during the passing of the bread and the cup should not be educational; otherwise, it will kill the Spirit. Any educational speaking for correction, instruction, or explanation should be given after the bread-breaking meeting. But we should avoid giving an educational word prior to and during the breaking of the bread, because it will distract the saints from the Lord. We should speak a word that will bring the saints into the Lord instead of out of the Lord.

Leading People to Appreciate the Sweetness and the Beauty of the Lord

When we began meeting in northern China, the word was ministered in every bread-breaking meeting. All the speaking was to lead people into the sweetness, glory, and beauty of the Lord. Once when we were about to break the bread, I stood up and shared a short word concerning the Lord being sweet and lovely to those who know and appreciate Him. I used various portions from the Gospels to show that the Lord was anointed on the head (Matt. 26:6-7), anointed on His feet (Luke 7:36-38), presented with frankincense and myrrh at His birth (Matt. 2:11), and anointed with spices for burial (John 19:39-40). Hence, from His head to His feet and from His birth to His death, the Lord is sweet and lovely. This speaking caused the brothers and sisters to know the Lord whom they were remembering.

In another bread-breaking meeting, I read from Isaiah 53: "He will see a seed, He will extend His days... / He will see the fruit of the travail of His soul, / And He will be satisfied" (vv. 10-11). Then I continued with a portion from the Psalms: "When I awake, I will be satisfied with Your likeness" (17:15). These two portions speak of satisfaction from two sides. In simple words I then explained, "Our gathering here is the issue of the Lord's labor; He is satisfied when He sees us. Not only so, when we come to the Lord's table, we are like those who have awakened from sleep. We are befuddled in the world, but when we come to the bread and the cup, we are awake. We are awake in Him, we behold His face, and we are satisfied. This is a story of satisfaction from two sides: we satisfy Him, and He satisfies us." Then I called a hymn related to this topic. We had numerous situations of this nature that were not educational but included a considerable amount of education.

On another occasion I stood up and said that the Lord was given a name which is above every name (Phil. 2:9). I then spoke for fifteen minutes concerning the Lord's name, showing the brothers and sisters that we are saved in this name, we have been placed into this name, we pray in this name, and we overcome Satan by this name. This speaking brought the saints into the Lord's name. After this we were all touched when we sang a hymn concerning the Lord's name.

In another bread-breaking meeting I spoke on the bread and the cup. It was a simple message showing that the bread is a story of life and the cup is a story of blessing. The Lord's life, symbolized by the bread, is for our enjoyment. Also, God Himself and all that He is have become our blessing in the cup. In an earlier message I focused on the cup and began speaking on the significance of the cup according to Psalm 16:5, which says, "Jehovah is the portion...of my cup." A cup signifies the portion we should have. Originally, our portion was the cup of God's wrath. This portion is the lake of fire. Revelation 14 speaks of a group of people whose portion is the lake of fire burning with brimstone (v. 10). The portion that God measured out for them is the lake of fire, the cup of His wrath. When the Lord went to the cross, He took the cup of God's wrath. The Lord said, "The cup which the Father has given Me, shall I not drink it?" (John 18:11). He drank the cup of wrath for us. Because the fire of God's wrath was burning Him when He was dying on the cross, He said He was thirsty. This corresponds to the Lord's words in Psalm 22: "All my bones are out of joint. / My heart is like wax; / It is melted within me... / My tongue is stuck to my jaws" (vv. 14-15). This describes the Lord's thirst. On the cross the Lord's blood was shed, which constitutes the cup of salvation for us, and this cup runs over with blessing.

As we remember Him, when we see the cup, we should realize that He drank the cup of wrath, which was our portion, on our behalf. He then gave us the cup of salvation that runs over with blessing. When we break the bread to remember the Lord, we are receiving the cup of blessing. If we speak concerning the bread and the cup in the fellowship meeting or prayer meeting, our speaking will not draw people's attention, but when we speak of them during the bread-breaking meeting, our speaking becomes very attractive.

We should not speak in an educational way concerning the Lord Jesus' person and work in the bread-breaking meeting; instead, we should speak in an ordinary way with love. We should speak like someone telling a love story. We are saying how wonderful the person is whom we love. For example, we can read a portion from Song of Songs describing Him as "dazzling white yet ruddy, / Distinguished among ten thousand" (5:10). We can then say something concerning *white* and *ruddy*. We should also point out the Lord's beauty and loveliness so that others can have a real and sweet knowledge of Him. The bread-breaking meeting is to remember the Lord's work and to glorify and exalt His name. Therefore, we can even say something concerning His return. Since the Lord's table implies His coming again, this word can be very sweet. As often as we eat the bread and drink the cup, we declare the Lord's death until He comes (1 Cor. 11:26). The Lord said that after He drank the cup with His disciples, He would not drink it again until that day when He would drink it new with them in the kingdom of His Father (Matt. 26:29). A short word can bring saints into the Lord's coming. While the saints remember the Lord, they are awaiting His coming. A word given from a heart full of feeling stirs people up.

Needing the Supply
through the Ministry of the Word

Every believer loves the Lord. When his love for the Lord is stirred up, he will look forward to the next bread-breaking meeting. If he receives a taste and a supply, he will surely want to come again. If every brother and sister were like the apostle Paul, there would be no need for us to stir up their heart. But many of the saints are new believers who truly need the help and the supply. If they come to the meeting time after time, but they do not know how to sing hymns and pray like others, they can only listen to others. If they continually hear the same tunes, they will feel that the meeting is tasteless, long, and tedious. Sometimes an entire meeting is like an elderly person going down the stairs; it causes people to break out in a cold sweat and nobody knows what to do. Such meetings cannot uplift people's spirit or satisfy them. It cannot make them willing to pay the price to come to the meeting again.

Therefore, we cannot complain about any decrease in the attendance in meetings. Those who take the lead in the meetings, particularly those who minister the word, bear the main responsibility. We need to minister the word in all the meetings to supply and give instruction to the saints. For example, after the new believers in northern China received help in fundamental matters for five years, their prayer and praise in the bread-breaking meeting was able to render much help to other new believers. They praised the Lord for His sweetness and for the fruit of His labor, declaring that they were satisfied with Him. These saints prayed, "Lord, You are so sweet. From Your head to Your feet You are worthy to be anointed by us. Lord, from Your birth to Your death You are worthy to be anointed. Lord, You are satisfied when You see the fruit of Your labor. Today we are sitting in Your presence, and we are satisfied when we look upon You." Many people became open when they heard such prayers. In some prayers there is a supply through the ministering of the word. Prayers that are full of light can render a supply to others.

If our bread-breaking meeting does not supply people through the ministry of the word, it is very poor. New believers will feel that the meeting is meaningless if they do not gain much nor hear any speaking with spiritual content. We should not only stand on the proper ground but also be in a normal condition.

To Serve in the Ministry of the Word Requiring One to Spend Time to Study

Those who minister the word should spend time before the Lord daily, studying how to minister the word in the bread-breaking meeting. Our speaking in the bread-breaking meeting is not the same as speaking from the podium. It should not be educational in nature; rather, it should be with feeling, causing people to see the Lord's beauty, to appreciate and worship Him, and to be drawn to Him. Our speaking should not cause them to forget the Lord. On the contrary, our speaking should cause them to see the Lord and enter into His presence. We should speak concerning the Lord's work and person, His exaltation, His name, His glory, and His second coming. We might even say something concerning His power, but this depends on how we speak. We should always speak with feeling, touching on the fact that God's love is with power and that His power is manifested in His love. Such speaking is very sweet.

If we merely say that the Lord's power is great, even greater than atomic energy, the brothers and sisters may forget His loveliness. For this reason, we should consider the way we speak. We may say, "The Lord's power is in His love. Some mothers love their children but do not have the power to properly care for them. But our Lord is not like this. There is power in His love, and His power is manifested through His love." When we speak in this way, the saints feel that the Lord is both lovely and powerful. They will be brought to the Lord and into the Lord. Moreover, this kind of speaking will not interrupt the spirit of worship in the saints.

When we speak, we should pay attention to the atmosphere in the meeting. Sometimes we should speak at the beginning of the meeting or when the bread and cup are being passed. It is extraordinary and full of meaning when our words follow the bread as it is being passed. When the brothers and sisters are passing the bread, we speak concerning the bread; after the bread has been passed around, we can speak concerning the cup. This will give the saints a sweet taste. They will not feel that we are speaking. Rather, they will sense an atmosphere that brings them before the Lord. They may have the sweet feeling that the Lord is shedding His blood in their presence and that the flow of His blood is for them to drink. The supply provided by such a speaking is full of taste. This shows that speaking for the Lord requires a considerable amount of study.

THE MINISTRY OF THE WORD REQUIRING ABSOLUTE DEDICATION

For this reason, those who administrate the church and minister the word cannot be simple persons. We should dedicate our whole being to what we are doing. This can be compared to an experienced engineer who is continually considering the design of a building. Even when he is sleeping, he is considering the design. Thus, it is not simple for him to design a project. However, it seems as if we consider our service to be simple.

For example, the responsible brothers usually arrive at the bread-breaking meeting when it is time to start. They do not consider how to lead the meeting until the meeting has already begun. It is at this moment that they begin to think about choosing a hymn, and one of them looks for a hymn, flipping through the hymnal from page to page. After the hymn is sung, it is followed with a prayer, then the singing of another hymn. This situation gives the saints the feeling that the leading ones are killing time. After the bread and the cup are passed, a brother may then stand up and say that he has something to fellowship, but because he did not spend the time to prepare, no one understands what he is saying.

Those who are responsible for the meetings should not feel at peace if there is no supply in the bread-breaking meeting. They should not be able to eat or sleep. All the time they should be considering how to improve the meeting. They should not be able to sleep peacefully. This is the proper attitude of those who are responsible for the meeting.

Some complain that there is not enough material to compose a message. When I began serving the Lord, there was no material, and there was no one to help me. When we first held the bread-breaking meeting, we simply broke the bread.

But as I considered this matter, I felt that we should abandon the routines of the denominations. After much consideration I received light, and we found the way to go on. I spent a long time searching, because I did not have peace. For example, I considered, "Should the prayer meeting be done in this way? When Christians come together to pray, is this the way to do it?" If we think in this way, I believe that the Lord will let us know what we should do.

The brothers and sisters need to know the meaning of prayer, what to pray for, and how to pray in a meeting. This should be according to the Bible. Then we need to find something to minister to them. If we do this, the prayer meeting will change, and the number of those attending the meetings will increase. The saints will enjoy coming to the prayer meeting because they receive the supply. This matter requires much thought. The more we endeavor, the more living the prayer meeting will become.

A SPECIAL COMMISSION TO THOSE SERVING IN THE MINISTRY OF THE WORD

Those who serve in the ministry of the word should study how to minister the word in the bread-breaking meeting and in the prayer meeting. We should minister the word in the prayer meeting without being long or killing the spirit of prayer and disrupting the mood for prayer. On the contrary, our speaking should strengthen and open the spirit of prayer and stir others up to pray. It is positive if those who do not normally pray would pray after we release the word.

When I first went to Manila, the brothers and sisters feared the prayer meeting and the bread-breaking meeting even though these two meetings are the most important in the Christian life. For this reason, I requested the responsible brothers to set up a bread-breaking meeting that would be held in the evening. The responsible brothers felt that no one would come if the meeting was in the evening. I endeavored to adjust them, and eventually the bread-breaking meeting had the best attendance. Presently, the number of saints attending the bread-breaking meeting in Manila is more than those who attend the Lord's Day morning meeting. The saints say that it is because there is a supply in the bread-breaking meeting.

Regrettably, I was not able to labor for a long period there. Hence, the effect of my labor did not match what we did in northern China. We were successful in northern China because we labored for many years, and we concentrated on only one local church. In Manila, however, there were many matters to attend to, and it was not appropriate for me to take over a local church and do the work by myself. I could serve only as an adviser. In spite of these reasons, there was still improvement.

We should all practice the matters that we have fellowshipped. We should not pay attention only to the speaking on the Lord's Day morning. We should endeavor to uplift the bread-breaking meeting. We should also raise the level of the prayer meeting. There must be the supply of the word in these meetings. We should study how to supply a specific word. We need to dig out the gold and find the treasures.

LEARNING TO ADJUST THE MEETING

Furthermore, we should lead the saints to take part in the activities in the meetings. This requires a certain amount of study. For example, when should we select a hymn? When and how should the announcements be given? When should everyone stand to sing, and when should they kneel down to sing? These matters require careful consideration. Sometimes our kneeling down to sing can uplift a meeting, or our standing to sing can revive the spirit. This is a mysterious matter.

We should not be legal regarding standing or sitting. Sometimes the way a person stands in the meeting can become monotonous, but if we criticize him, he might not be willing to stand in the meeting for another six months. We should not be rigid. Sometimes our body needs to sit, stand, walk, or lie down. For this reason, there should be some who can appropriately lead and adjust the meetings. However, those who adjust are not replacing the brothers and sisters; rather, they are helping them. The Holy Spirit often moves through people. If there is no one to adjust the meeting, it may be difficult for the spirit of the brothers and sisters to be uplifted.

If the spirit is adjusted, the spirit can be enlivened. Hence, we should learn to follow the spirit.

We need to learn how to adjust and uplift the prayer meeting and the bread-breaking meeting. This applies to the fellowship meeting and other meetings as well. We are responsible to supply brothers and sisters with the word. In other words, there should always be someone who follows the Holy Spirit to adjust the meeting. There should also be a short ministering of the word to render help to the saints. After attending such a meeting, the saints will be willing to come again. As long as they desire to gain the Lord and are able to receive the spiritual supply in the meetings, they will want to come to the meetings. I hope that the brothers and sisters will pay attention to this matter.

CHAPTER TWELVE

THE WORD BEING TO SUPPLY AND ADMINISTRATION BEING FOR BUILDING UP

CARING FOR PRACTICAL NEEDS IN GIVING MESSAGES, NOT PROFUNDITY

In the previous chapter we considered our need to study how to use the ministry of the word to uplift the meetings of the church. In addition, the ministry of the word should be living and practical; it does not depend on lofty subjects and deep content. We should not think that subjects such as regeneration and dealing with sins are too shallow simply because others have already spoken on these subjects. This concept is very wrong. The ministry of the word depends on the need. If some need to hear a message on regeneration, we should give a living word. I believe that even the apostle Paul sometimes liked to hear others preaching the gospel; he probably received the supply through their gospel preaching, because the preaching was living.

Some brothers feel that it is not easy to give a message in the church in Taipei, because the saints have heard good and high messages in the conferences. If the speaking is on a common subject, the saints have heard it, but if the speaking is on a high subject, the saints cannot come up to the standard. In ministering the word, the content should not be too high. It is wrong to go to the "high places" to find a way. It is not normal to walk on the rooftops. Those who try to walk on rooftops are looking for trouble. Rather, we should always choose a clear and unobstructed way when we walk, and since there would be no obstructions, the way can be taken repeatedly. Hence, we should not be afraid of old subjects; we should be afraid only of old utterances and old ways of speaking. The topic can be the same, but there must be different ways to present it so that it will be living. There is no profit in our striving for extra lofty messages. We should believe that among the ministers raised up by God in the church, some will function to supply the church with fresh and original things, and others will not.

The brothers and sisters do not need profound words in order to be supplied; they simply need ordinary words in order for them to be supplied. Ones are being saved every day, and they need to know how to consecrate themselves. Those who have already consecrated themselves, however, need to refresh their consecration. Therefore, we do not necessarily need to give lofty messages. We need to labor to receive a burden from the Lord. We should hold to this principle. We must see the need of the brothers and sisters. Instead of caring for whether a message is shallow or deep, we should care for the genuine need of the church. The speaking in regular meetings is always different from the speaking in the conferences. Conferences release messages at specified times to sow the need of the church into the saints. The saints should digest these messages. The speaking on the Lord's Day, however, is to meet the general needs of the brothers and sisters. Hence, there is no need to consider whether the message is shallow or deep, and there is also no need to be concerned that it has been spoken by others. Our only concern should be whether it meets the need of the brothers and sisters. For a message to meet the need, our words must be living.

We should never be afraid that a common subject is too shallow for the saints. Actually, there is no such thing as a shallow message. Even a shallow message can minister deep things into people. In 1942 a brother who was meeting in a denomination often came to our meetings in order to hear the gospel messages. Even though the gospel is a very simple message by which unbelievers are saved, this brother eventually turned to the ground of the church because of these gospel messages. Those who bear the responsibility of the ministry of the word should have a change in concept. We should not consider whether a topic is profound or simple or whether others have already spoken on it. Instead of considering such matters, we should receive a burden to see exactly what the brothers and sisters need. Once we receive a burden, we should study to find a living way to present it. This does not mean that our words need to be lively, fluent, or persuasive but rather that we should speak words of life to touch, move, and uplift the spirit of the saints and to convict them in their spirit, thereby setting them free. This is where we should spend our energy and effort.

Hence, we need to fervently pray: "Lord, today I am speaking on regeneration. You must give me a fresh and living word." Our speaking should be such that even the apostle Paul would say that our speaking touched his inner being. Our speaking should render even experienced believers a supply that is as fresh, cool, and watering as the morning dew. Even though regeneration is an "old" topic that has been spoken about many times, we should still give people a fresh supply in their spirit. This is the living word.

THE MINISTRY OF THE WORD HAVING A MAIN POINT AND SUPPLYING THE SAINTS

As those who are responsible for the ministry of the word in the local churches, we should learn to have a main point and at the same time be able to supply the word in all aspects. No one should say that he can only preach the gospel. We should seek out how to lead the responsible ones in the homes and in the small groups. We must seek to have a word for these responsible brothers, and we must seek to have a word to supply all the needs of the saints.

We are focused in our ministry of the word. We can speak concerning Christ, the Son of God, the cross, dealing with the flesh, and other topics that supply the saints. However, we also need words that can take care of the serving ones. Although the speaking in a local church may have Christ, the Son of God, the cross, and the dealing with the flesh as the focus, there is also the need for speaking concerning other aspects. For instance, if we eat beef in the morning and in the evening, sooner or later we will be in trouble. Since human beings need nutrition from different vitamins, we need all kinds of food. Not only so, the northern Chinese like garlic, and the Westerners like coffee. Some like soy sauce, and others like vinegar with their meals. We must learn how to supply the various needs of the saints; otherwise, the saints will know only one truth, and they will become unbalanced. Thus, the church will suffer a great loss.

When the brothers and sisters are strong in a certain item but weak in other items, it is difficult for the church to advance. We can speak on the same point if we are ministering to many churches and not caring for only one church. If I am in Tainan for two months, I can concentrate on serving the saints the subject of dealing with the flesh. If I then go to Taichung for another two months, I can serve the saints the same thing. This is acceptable, because every church needs to learn how to deal with the flesh. But it is not acceptable to stay in one locality and speak every year concerning dealing with the flesh. Such speaking will cause the church to become unbalanced.

Therefore, those who minister the word need to learn to be versatile. This is similar to a military expert who is also capable of handling financial matters and a financier who is also good with educational issues. An economist who specializes in economics and knows nothing about military affairs cannot lead an army. General Tseng Kuo-fan was a literary writer, but he was able to overturn the rebellious government called the Heavenly Kingdom of Peace. He combined military tactics with politics and therefore succeeded in winning the victory. Hence, no one should say that he can speak only about the cross and specialize in dealing with the flesh.

Those who stress dealing with the flesh should learn to preach the gospel and to teach the brothers and sisters how to function in the meetings. We should be multifaceted; otherwise, the church will be unbalanced. A good housewife can prepare many different dishes. Even though carrots are good, she does not serve only carrots every day. Similarly, we should not speak on dealing with the flesh in every meeting. We should speak concerning prayer in the prayer meeting, concerning worship in the bread-breaking meeting, concerning service in the fellowship meeting, and concerning bearing responsibility to a small group of saints who bear many burdens in the service. In these various meetings the ministry of the word is supplementary. The main focus may be how to deal with the flesh and to know Christ, but it is still necessary to supply the word in other aspects.

The church should not have supplemental speaking without focused speaking. We need to take care of both. This principle applies to the Bible. No book covers only one subject. For instance, although the book of Romans focuses on justification by faith, it also has a greeting in the beginning, a blessing in the end, and many other aspects of the truth, such as presenting our bodies and receiving the saints. These aspects have nothing to do with justification by faith, yet they are attached to justification by faith, the central message. The book of Ephesians is profound, but it includes topics concerning honoring parents, submitting to husbands, loving wives, not letting the sun go down on one's indignation, and stealing no more (6:1; 5:22, 25, 33; 4:26, 28). This book focuses on the church being the Body of Christ, the fullness of the One who fills all in all (1:23), but there are many other supplemental topics.

In the church we are building up the Body of Christ; hence, we focus on helping people know the all-inclusive Christ, the cross, and dealing with the flesh. But our speaking should also supply the many other needs of the saints. Sometimes there is a practical need for a word of comfort or a word on suffering even though such a word is not as important as the central message. For instance, after praying in a prayer meeting for a family who was going through some trials and for some brothers and sisters who were unemployed or sick, I used the remaining ten minutes to speak concerning sufferings and trials. This comforted and encouraged the hearers. They then shared those words with their family so that the family was also encouraged and strengthened.

This shows that the ministry of the word should be living and multifaceted. We should never think that after giving a message on the Lord's Day, our burden is gone, and we can relax until Thursday night when we again go "to the cross" and speak. This is not acceptable. We must learn to be versatile to meet various needs. We might not have considered speaking on afflictions, but because we heard the prayers of the brothers and sisters in the prayer meeting and saw the tears shed for the suffering and sorrow of a family, we may realize that there is a need. Consequently, after the prayer meeting, we should rise up to share a word according to inspiration. Such inspiration is a result of daily exercise. The Spirit of God cannot move a stone. We must be constituted by reading verses or messages concerning suffering. Then when we feel in our spirit that the brothers and sisters need such a word, we will be able to comfort, strengthen, and instruct them in their suffering. This requires much preparation.

One does not become a renowned actor, singer, or musician overnight. One must devote his entire being in order to become successful and famous. An actor must study how to walk and how to laugh. He must learn to laugh so that his laughter touches the feeling of others. Then when he laughs on the stage, the audience will be touched with the same feeling and also laugh. When he cries on the stage, the audience will also cry. But this skill cannot be acquired in a month. He must daily spend the time to study, practice, and learn from the famous performers of the past and the present. He needs to learn from them and add his own ideas to produce something new. In this way he can create a unique style of his own.

I am not encouraging us to become great teachers; rather, my desire is that we endeavor to do things in a respectable manner. We should never think that because our truths are rich, we have enough content for one hundred and four weeks. If we think this way, we will become sloppy and perfunctory. Instead, we should spend time to daily consider and study the condition of the brothers and sisters and the situation of the church. We should not merely copy the messages that were given by others without studying. If we endeavor to study, we will exercise our spirit, receive a burden, and minister to people according to the need. When we exercise our spirit in a wedding meeting, we will know the need of the couple and share a word to meet the need. When we are in a memorial service, we will know whether the family needs comforting or strengthening and supply them accordingly. Such an exercise requires much preparation.

Our ministry of the word should have a focus, and we should be versatile. We need to learn how to minister the word to meet different needs. We should not regard this as an easy matter. When we minister the word, we must always have a focus, and we must take care of the various needs. Otherwise, our ministry will be unbalanced, and the church will suffer a great loss. Since most of the co-workers stay in one place, taking care of one locality, the ministry of the word must cover many aspects, or the church will suffer a loss.

THE MANNER OF SPEAKING NEEDING TO BE FITTING AND PROPER

Those who release the word must learn to pay attention also to their manner of speaking. This refers to posture and is related to our temperament. Of course, we do not pay attention to outward things, but the way we speak can greatly affect the release of the word. It is possible for our posture to reduce the weight of our message. For example, too many hand gestures can be distracting and should be corrected. We can correct this by practicing to speak in front of a mirror. Then we will know how to correct ourselves.

A worker of the Lord should not pretend; however, every worker should maintain proper deportment. Deportment refers to one's manner of speaking. The first lesson a diplomat must learn is deportment. A diplomat cannot act like a child in the midst of a major event. Even an athlete maintains proper deportment. He has a certain bearing whether he is walking or running. When an athlete stands, he has a certain bearing that enables others to recognize that he is an athlete.

A worker should never pretend but be genuine. Nevertheless, we should have proper deportment. The sisters should have a bearing that is proper for a sister. This is different from the bearing of a brother. The elderly ones should have a deportment that is appropriate to them. The same applies to new ones. Some elders are careless when they contact the saints; they do not have proper deportment. An elder should not carry himself like a bureaucrat, being special and above others. An elder should behave becomingly. He should be sincere, unpretentious, and artless, not putting on airs. At the same time he should be neither light nor loose. People should feel that he is weighty and that he has the deportment of an elder. These qualities are related to a person's birth, disposition, education, environment, and family background.

Every diplomat needs to learn three important lessons. He must first learn proper deportment. Then he must improve his language ability. A diplomat must be good with words. He should be able to turn any situation around with a few words. We are all ambassadors of the kingdom of God, diplomats, who interact with the devil's kingdom on earth every day. We have had the experience of turning those who oppose us with just a few words. They even receive the Lord after a few words even though they initially had no desire for Him. Therefore, the second thing a diplomat must learn is how to speak.

Third, a diplomat must learn magnanimity. A magnanimous person does not necessarily let others know when he is happy or sad. A magnanimous person always allows others to retreat. For instance, when he is offended, he does not immediately become angry. Instead, he exercises magnanimity to withdraw and consider the situation to see if he has the basis to give a clear response. He does not become angry immediately after he has been offended, nor is he willing to do things for others based on his mood. A magnanimous diplomat always consults many experts, such as his advisors, supervisors, secretaries, and counselors to examine the advantages and disadvantages of a situation before responding.

A person who cannot learn these three matters cannot become a good diplomat even if he has a wealth of knowledge. Knowledge is secondary for a diplomat. The most important matter is his deportment. Then he must have an ability to speak and to be magnanimous. When he is provoked, he will not lose his temper, and when he is praised, he will not freely oblige others. Every serving one should learn these three matters. It is absolutely inappropriate for us to lose our temper when we are offended by a brother. It is also not suitable for us to readily agree to a brother's request when he is favorable to us.

We must pay attention to our deportment when we contact others and when we minister the word. It is rather difficult for others to correct us in this matter. It is best for us to stand before a mirror, observe ourselves, and make the necessary corrections. For example, there is a brother who always frowns, with one eyebrow cocked high and the other low, when he stands up to speak. Then he shakes his head twice before he utters his first sentence. This brother has been doing this for more than twenty years. He has never changed his deportment in speaking throughout all these years. There is another brother who is often nervous and excited when he receives foreign guests, and even though he is warm, his behavior is unbecoming. It is possible to remain calm and dignified when we shake hands. If we behave unbecomingly, we give others a poor impression.

Furthermore, we should not all have the same posture when we speak. For example, there was a preacher who wore a robe and did not move much when he spoke, but when he opened his mouth to say "For God so loved the world...," it was full of touching power. Another preacher would run down from the platform, around the meeting hall, and then back up to the platform when giving a message. He would cry and laugh, shout and yell, and kneel or lie down. Sometimes he would mimic the way women walk and the way they talk to show that it was unbecoming. People usually found it difficult to accept his behavior, but after listening to the message, they were subdued and conceded that his behavior was right; it was not unbecoming. Therefore, every one who ministers the word has his own deportment.

This matter of deportment is a problem to nearly everyone. Ten years ago there was a brother who continually lifted his trousers while speaking. Another brother was oblivious to the fact that his belt was crooked whenever he finished speaking. Still another brother liked to grab his tie when he spoke. Although these are not important issues, they can affect our speaking of the word. A brother who likes to frown should not speak in a wedding meeting or a memorial service. Weddings are happy occasions, and his frowning would not be appropriate. Likewise, people are sad enough in a memorial service; they do not need his frowns. In fact, it is unseemly for such a person to speak in any occasion.

Some people always have an appropriate deportment. On a happy occasion their speaking is proper even though they do not speak concerning happiness. When they speak in a memorial meeting, the relatives of the deceased are greatly comforted. They may not speak much, but their deportment has much weight.

At one time I thought that Brother Nee was too spiritual to pay attention to a matter as small as appearance. One day, however, as he was teaching me how to typeset hymns in Chinese, he said that if we printed the hymns horizontally, they would be less effective in touching people, but if we printed them vertically, there would be more impact. We then typeset a hymn horizontally and vertically. When we read and sang the hymn, we found that there was indeed a difference. As human beings, we are affected by many things. The ability to touch people is basically the work of the Holy Spirit; however, certain things can frustrate this work. Reading something horizontally can frustrate this work whereas reading the same thing vertically can assist this work. In the same way, proper deportment not only removes people's resistance to the Holy Spirit but also assists the work of the Spirit. If our deportment is poor, it will become a cause of resistance to the Holy Spirit. Sometimes our poor deportment can completely nullify the impact of our speaking. When people do not like our deportment, they do not listen to what we say; their heart is closed, and they cannot receive anything from the message.

In addition, young people should never behave like old people. They should be proper and natural, maintaining an appropriate and proper deportment. We should be beside ourselves before God and sober-minded before men (2 Cor. 5:13). However, being sober before our parents is different from being sober before our children. Even though we are sober, our behavior is different. Being sober before our parents expresses one kind of deportment, but the deportment before our children is different. We need to study this matter.

THE ADMINISTRATION OF THE CHURCH BEING MAINLY FOR BUILDING UP

In the administration of the church, there is one matter that has been neglected by all the churches. In our understanding, the administration of the church is related to the administration of business affairs. Some may even understand that administration means to administrate, to manage people. Even though this is not wrong, it is not the real meaning of the administration of the church. The administration of the church is mainly for the building up of the believers corporately, not individually. The administration of the church is mainly to build many individuals up together. Where there is no administration, there is no building, but if there is administration, there is also a need to build people up together.

How should the administration be carried out in order for there to be the building up? The twelve elders in the church in Taipei may arrange to have twenty-eight brothers responsible for the group meetings. To a certain extent such an arrangement is focused on building, especially if there are brothers and sisters who love the Lord and pursue spirituality but have no practical coordination among themselves. In order to have practical coordination, there is a need for the administration of the church. But the elders should not stop at appointing responsible brothers who could bear responsibility for the home meeting. This administration clearly has the nature of building. However, they should advance.

The elders may observe that a brother who should be responsible for a group meeting has problems that need to be taken care of; otherwise, he will be unable to bear responsibility with others in the future. The elders should spend time considering this brother, praying for him and fellowshipping with him. They should continue in prayer and fellowship until they are able to speak with this brother concerning the problems. If this brother receives the fellowship, the problems will be removed, and there will be no problems when he coordinates with others for the group meeting. This is building.

This can be compared to building with stones. In order for one stone to be upon another, the bottom stone must be flat. Any part of the stone that protrudes needs to be ground away in order for another stone to be secure when it is placed on top of it. This shows that building involves more than placing one stone upon another. It also involves removing the protruding parts of a stone so that it can be built upon another. This is the meaning of administration. When those who administrate the church see that a brother who could bear responsibility is lacking something, they should make up the lack for him. This can also be compared to looking for stones to build a house. A suitable stone may have a protruding edge that needs to be ground away. Then the stone can be built upon others securely.

It may also be that a responsible brother may not speak much and may not be apt to minister the word, but his administration in the meeting can still have the flavor of building. He observes the brothers and sisters and knows when they are ready to bear responsibility or when they need some training. Eventually the saints in his meeting will be able to bear some responsibility. This is building, and this is administration. Therefore, the elders should spend one-fourth of their meeting time to discuss business affairs and three-fourths of the time to discuss the condition of the brothers and sisters. They should not gossip about the strengths and shortcomings of the saints. Rather, they should study the saints to know if they are fulfilling their duties or have problems. There may be a brother who seems to be very useful, but he has a problem. Likewise, another brother may be able to minister the word, but he is not mature enough to be a deacon. Consequently, the elders should consider the best way to help these brothers. An elder may be burdened to spend six months with them so that they may be perfected and continue to function in the ministry of the word. This type of administration of the church has value and weight. Administration does not merely deal with business affairs. It is to build the believers up.

Regrettably, our administration of the church is still lacking. When a saint has a problem, the elders should study the situation and take care of it according to the building. If the problem is not properly taken care of, other saints will also have problems, and the building will be frustrated.

When I bore responsibility in a local church in northern

China, we did much in the aspect of administrating the church. Material offerings were also included in the administration of the church. We did not give our offerings indiscriminately. The giving was done under the leading of the administration of the church, ensuring that the recipient would truly benefit from the offering. The way we render help to a needy brother is part of the administration. This is what elders should do. Elders are shepherds, teachers, and administrators. These three functions are interrelated and should not be separated. Some brothers are good at handling business affairs, and some are good at perfecting the saints. However, the elders should not work separately; they should coordinate together as one person to observe all the sides of a situation. When the majority of the time and energy in the elders' meeting, which is for the administration of the church, is spent on business affairs, the church suffers a loss, because the spiritual needs of the saints are not touched. When the administration of the church does not touch the spirit of the saints, the church suffers a loss.

Three-fourths of the time and energy in the elders' meeting should be spent on the spiritual situation of the saints. We cannot do without the business aspect of the administration of the church, but we need more practice on how much to use our time on it. Administrating the spiritual needs of the saints requires much more effort and time than the mere management of business affairs. It requires our patience, wisdom, and strong will to do everything in love, not according to natural affection. This can be compared to the situation of a doctor and a patient. A doctor prescribes what his patient needs in love. When the patient needs medication, he prescribes it; if the patient needs an operation, he performs it. Therefore, in the administration of the church, the elders should learn when to be soft, hard, quick, and slow. They should be balanced in every situation. They should not handle every situation the same way. One situation may require severity, and another may require leniency. All of these matters require learning.

Leading people to salvation does not require much learning. Likewise, edifying people does not require much learning. However, if we desire to administrate the church and to minister the word to build up the children of God for the manifestation of God's dwelling place and the functioning of the Body of Christ, we need to learn many lessons. If we do not learn the lessons, we may save sinners and perfect the saints but be unable to build them up to be the Body of Christ, the dwelling place of God. It is even possible that we ourselves will not be built up. If this is the case, we can serve as elders or in the ministry of the word, but our administration of the church and our ministering of the word can only cause the saints to love the Lord zealously and be individually spiritual. It cannot build them up together to be filled with the presence of God inwardly and the authority of God outwardly so that they become the dwelling place of God, the Body of Christ, God's desire. If we endeavor to properly carry out the administration of the church, the power and effect of our gospel will increase, and the effect of our edification of the saints will also increase.

THE BUILT-UP CHURCH HASTENING THE LORD'S RETURN

God's blessing is in the Body, His dwelling place. This is the age of grace. God gives grace to all believers even to those who are Catholic. He causes His sun to rise on the evil and the good, and He sends rain on the just and the unjust (Matt. 5:45); this is grace. But we cannot say that the believers in Catholicism can satisfy God's heart's desire and need in this age. In the same principle, we can save many people and perfect them to become spiritual, but this cannot satisfy the desire of God's heart. The desire of God's heart is to obtain a built-up Body in this age. This is what He is doing.

If God's chosen ones are not built up today, they will still need to be built up one day. There are no scattered believers in the new heaven and new earth. Rather, all the believers are built together into a city in which the foundations and wall are precious stones, and the gates are pearls. We should not wait for the future to be built. We might not know how to be built, but God wants His believers to be built. God tells us clearly that after we are saved, we should be built. We are the house built by God (Eph. 2:22; 1 Pet. 2:5). God gives different gifts for the building up of the Body (Eph. 4:11-12). If we earnestly desire gifts, we should desire the gift of building up the church. God desires a dwelling place, a Body, but He has encountered many difficulties during the past two thousand years. It is not difficult to lead people to salvation; it is also not difficult to help them to be spiritual. However, it is truly difficult to build up a group of people as a spiritual Body, a corporate dwelling place. For this reason, not much building has taken place in church history.

Brother T. Austin-Sparks once asked me my feeling concerning the Lord's second coming. I responded that my inward feeling was that the Lord's coming was not yet near. According to Revelation 14:15, the harvest of the earth needs to ripen so that it can be reaped. The ripened harvest and the imminent reaping refer to the Lord's reaping of His mature believers at His coming. However, God's people, His harvest, are not ripe. There are only tender shoots. The Lord of the harvest cannot return when there is nothing to reap. This matter involves the rapture of the believers and the maturity of life. If the church aggressively pursues the building up, the believers will mature sooner, and the Lord of the harvest can return to reap the harvest. Those who grow rice know that everyone likes to harvest early if the rice is ripened. However, if the fields are still green, there is no way to harvest.

Two thousand years ago the Lord said, "Behold, I come quickly" (22:7, 12). He desires to come back, but the harvest on earth is not ripe. How can He come before the harvest is ripe? Revelation 14:15 does not depend on a timetable; it depends on life. The quicker our life matures, the sooner the Lord will return. If we require a longer time to mature in life, the Lord will return later. From the aspect of maturity in life, the church is full of green fields and even desolation. Because there is no building, those who are enlightened will mourn over the desolate situation; they will not rejoice. What makes us most sorrowful is the condition of the church with regard to building. We mourn daily for this because no one speaks concerning the building up of the church and because there is not much building among us. Surely we should pay attention to the propagation of the work, but we should pay even more attention to the building. Otherwise, the Lord has no way, and our work has no way. If we do not have a way, the saints do not have a way.

Now is the time when we urgently need the building. Since we are attending to the Lord's work, in everything we do, whether in the administration of the church, the ministry of the word, or visiting the saints, we should hold on to the principle that our work should result in the building up of the believers. We should be able to build the believers up one by one into the Body of Christ, into a corporate vessel of God on earth. God desires a corporate vessel, not an individual vessel. If our desire is merely to edify people for their individual spirituality, there is not much more for us to learn. However, if we desire to participate in the work of the building, there are many lessons to learn, and we need to be corrected in many areas. Our administration of the church needs to be corrected, our ministry of the word needs to be corrected, and the way we visit people needs to be corrected. We need to diligently learn the lessons. There is not much of the element of building in our administration of the church and our ministry of the word.

From now on, the administration in all the churches should focus on people, not only on business affairs. We should focus on all the believers, not on specific individuals, so that they might become a corporate vessel. We are being built up in our coordination with others, and we are learning how to administrate and help others. We will learn to make up the lack in some and remove the excess from others, or add to those who have little function and help those who already function to develop in their function even more. We will also learn to help others to coordinate so that there will be no spiritual individuals who manifest their function individualistically. Instead, all the believers should be joined together to manifest their function in coordination. By doing this, we will prepare an excellent way for the Lord to return.

THE BUILDING WORK NEEDING TO BE CARRIED OUT ON THE PROPER GROUND

In order for the Lord to advance in these last days, we cannot merely speak about the ground of the church. If we desire to have the building, we must be sure to have the proper ground. As long as our ground is uncertain, nothing can be worked out. We must also recognize the enemy's scheme. Without the proper ground, we can be spiritual, but we are in Babylon. We may be as spiritual as Daniel, but we will be unable to build up the holy temple. If we desire to be built together to become the holy temple, the holy city, we must return to Jerusalem. Therefore, we must be sure of the ground; otherwise, we will not know where to build. We can be spiritual in Babylon, Aram, Syria, and Samaria; we can be spiritual in a scattered way. However, the temple of God is not built in Babylon, Aram, Syria, or Samaria. It is built in Jerusalem. We cannot build according to individual opinions. We need to return to the foundation on which the forefathers built the temple—Jerusalem.

This matter is not according to our opinion. It is according to the light seen by the apostles. We should return to the same ground on which the apostles built the churches. All the things related to the church ground should be according to the Bible. This is similar to baptism. It is not a matter of baptism by sprinkling or by immersion but of returning to the practice in the beginning. In the beginning the saints were baptized in water. They were buried with Christ. Similarly, the practice of the Lord's table is not a matter of a big cup or a small cup but of returning to the practice in the beginning. The apostle Paul says, "Seeing that there is one bread, we who are many are one Body; for we all partake of the one bread" (1 Cor. 10:17). Though we are many, we are one bread. We must go back to the practice in the beginning.

In the beginning there was one ground of the church, the ground of locality. We must return to the Bible. The Bible speaks of the church in Jerusalem (Acts 8:1; 11:22), the church in Antioch (13:1), the church in Corinth (1 Cor. 1:2; 2 Cor. 1:1), and the church in Ephesus (Rev. 2:1). This shows the ground of the church. We cannot follow other proposals. We must have a definite ground, and then we can labor unreservedly to build up God's house. We can concentrate on the building work. We cannot speak of the building work if the ground is uncertain. We may speak about saving sinners and spiritual matters, but we cannot speak about the building.

We need to see both sides. We cannot have only the ground of the church. We must also have the building. However, if we lack the Lord's presence and His authority and if we are short of prayer and the dealing of the flesh, we will only have the local ground and nothing else. We need spiritual reality, and we also need the ground and the building. This is a twofold principle that we must grasp firmly.

The Lord raised us up with a great purpose. The ground of the church that we have taken has great impact on the children of God. We cannot lose our aim, neither should we forget our ministry and the work we are doing. If we are faithful on the ground to receive more dealings and to learn more lessons, relying on the Lord's grace to labor on the building, we will have great impact. Not only will we have the ground, but we also will have something solid and spiritual built on the ground. The impact of such a testimony to the church of God is beyond estimation, and the impact is even greater on the children of God. We believe that the Lord raised us up for this. Therefore, with our eyes bright and our goal clear, we must see what the Lord desires us to do. We need to see that in this age and in this universe, God intends to do a work of building, and this building work must be on a ground. We should stay on this ground, and keep up with God's leading today.

Chapter Thirteen

THE GROUND FOR THE BUILDING OF THE CHURCH

On the one hand, we need to see the building up of the church, and on the other hand, we need to see the main frustration to the building—not having the proper ground of the church. When the saints in Jerusalem were built together, they became the church in Jerusalem. Likewise, the saints in Ephesus were built up to be the church in Ephesus. However, the ground of the church is a serious problem today. In Taipei there are Baptist churches, Presbyterian churches, Lutheran churches, and other churches. Taipei has become a city of many churches.

THE GROUND OF THE BUILDING NOT DEPENDING ON THE MEASURE OF THE STATURE OF CHRIST

We need to build up the church and pay attention to the ground of the church. Brother T. Austin-Sparks thinks that the measure of the stature of Christ should be our criterion; that is, we should be able to join any group that has more Christ. The Catholic Church accepts the Bible, recognizes the Trinity, and confesses that Christ Jesus is the Son of God who was born of the virgin Mary, was crucified on the cross, shed His blood for our redemption, resurrected from the dead, and ascended to the heavens. These items are included in the orthodox belief of Catholicism. Some of the believers in Catholicism are more pious than many of us. Should we then join the Catholics since they have Christ? Or should we go to another group that has more Christ? What standard should one use to determine the amount of Christ that there is in a group?

THE GROUND OF THE CHURCH IN OUR BELIEF AND PRACTICE

A Western brother who was affected by Brother Austin-Sparks has asked why we say that only we are the church and that others are not. He is also questioning the local administration of the church. I shared three points with him. We believe that the church is uniquely one in the universe. We believe that the expression of the church in every city should also be one. The cities of Jerusalem, Antioch, and Corinth had only one expression, one church. We believe that any ground other than the local ground is sectarian and therefore should not exist.

SPIRITUAL REALITY AND THE GROUND OF THE CHURCH BEING TWO SEPARATE MATTERS

Brother Austin-Sparks does not agree with the ground of the church. He also condemns organized Christianity. In our time of fellowship with Brother Austin-Sparks, a brother asked, "If there are five independent groups in a city that have left organized Christianity, are any of these groups right or are they all wrong?" Brother Austin-Sparks replied that none of the groups were absolutely right, but that they were relatively right. When asked what he meant by relatively right, he said, "Each group should be measured according to the stature of Christ. The group that has a greater measure of the stature of Christ is more right; the group that has a smaller measure of the stature of Christ is less right."

I was the translator at the time, but at this juncture I joined the discussion. I asked whether there is any Christ in Catholicism. I then said that we have received help from Madame Guyon in the matter of life and that Madame Guyon definitely had a stature of Christ, but Madame Guyon was in Catholicism, which we condemn. We should be clear that spirituality and the ground of the church are two different matters. Madame Guyon was spiritual, but she was not right in the matter of the ground of the church. Dr. F. B. Meyer is highly recommended by Brother Austin-Sparks, but Dr. Meyer never left organized Christianity, which Brother Austin-Sparks condemned. Based on Dr. Meyer's spirituality and measure of Christ, should we say that organized Christianity is relatively correct? Andrew Murray is another spiritual giant who remained in organized Christianity. Therefore, we cannot determine the ground of the church based on a person's spirituality.

God desired that His people stay in the land of Israel and take Jerusalem as the center in their worshipping Him. Jerusalem was the ground for their worship of God. After being captive in Babylon for seventy years, there was a call for them to return to Jerusalem. What would have happened if at that time a prophet rose up and said that it did not matter whether they returned to Jerusalem or stayed in Babylon, because only their spiritual stature mattered? Daniel was the most spiritual among them. Using New Testament terms, Daniel was full of Christ, but such a Christ-filled, spiritual person remained in Babylon. Those who returned to Jerusalem were not as spiritual as Daniel. They had opinions and weaknesses, and some of them even married Gentile women. Their spiritual condition was far inferior to that of Daniel. However, was Daniel's ground correct, or was the ground of those who were weak and unspiritual correct? This shows that to be spiritual is one thing and that to have the proper ground of the church is another thing. A person may be very spiritual but stand on the wrong ground. Daniel's standing on the wrong ground was due to God's sovereign arrangement, not according to his own will. Although he was in Babylon, his heart was in Jerusalem.

One day Brother Austin-Sparks asked what we mean by *local ground*. I illustrated this with an example. I drew a circle that represented the city of Jerusalem and said that all the believers in Jerusalem met in that circle; hence, it was called the church in Jerusalem. The city of Jerusalem is the ground of the church in Jerusalem; the church is in Jerusalem. Then I drew another circle representing the church in Corinth. The church in Corinth was initially one, but the believers in Corinth became divided. Those who were for Paul became a Pauline sect. Suppose some in the Pauline sect moved to Samaria and declared that they belonged to Paul in

Samaria. They would be taking Paul as their ground instead of Samaria as their ground. Initially, there was only one church in Corinth—the church in Corinth. The city of Corinth was the ground of the church in Corinth. After they were divided, there were some of Paul, some of Apollos, some of Cephas, and some of Christ. They lost the local ground. The Pauline sect took Paul as their ground, and the Apollonian sect took Apollos as their ground. Suppose some brothers from the church in Jerusalem went to Samaria to meet with the brothers there only to discover that they belonged to Paul. The brothers in Jerusalem could explain that the church cannot be of Paul, but those in Samaria would insist on being of Paul; thus, the brothers from Jerusalem would have no alternative but to meet apart from them in Samaria. Although there would be two groups meeting in Samaria, one would be meeting on the local ground, and the other would be meeting on the ground of Paul.

It is possible that those who were on the proper ground were fleshly and that those who were on the ground of Paul were spiritual, each group had a measure of Christ. When other believers would go to Samaria, should they take the measure of Christ as the criterion and meet with the Pauline sect?

The next morning Brother Austin-Sparks spoke concerning Christ and said that we make Christ a small Christ and the church a small church by limiting everything to the ground. I calmly translated for him even though I felt uncomfortable within. This was a matter of the truth. Two plus two equals four. How can two plus two equal five? Brother Austin-Sparks also saw that we had come to an impasse, and he discontinued the fellowship meeting the next day. He said that he and another Western brother were satisfied with our replies and that there was no need to continue the discussion.

NOT GIVING UNDUE EMPHASIS
TO SPIRITUALITY AND THUS NEGLECTING
THE GROUND OF THE CHURCH

In order to build a house, there must be a site, the ground for the house. Similarly, the building of the church must have a ground. Brother Austin-Sparks overemphasizes spirituality

THE GROUND FOR THE BUILDING OF THE CHURCH 171

and neglects the ground. May the Lord cover me with His blood to say this: the work of Brother Austin-Sparks at Honor Oak is quite spiritual, but because he neglects the ground of the church, his work has no future. Those who meet in Honor Oak learn many spiritual matters and are helped spiritually. However, they have no place to go after they leave Honor Oak.

There was a good Brethren assembly in London; D. M. Panton also had a meeting there. Since these meetings were not in organized Christianity, why did Brother Austin-Sparks separate himself from them and begin another meeting in Honor Oak? This matter touches the ground. Brother Austin-Sparks may have said that those groups were not spiritual. If those groups are not spiritual, where should the brothers who meet with him go when they leave Honor Oak? Should they go to the Presbyterian Church, the Baptist Church, or should they follow the pattern of Brother Austin-Sparks and start another meeting? Spirituality is relative, but the ground is absolute.

Just as we received help from Madame Guyon and honor her spiritual portion, we also received help from Brother Austin-Sparks and respect his spiritual portion. However, we disagree with Madame Guyon and Brother Austin-Sparks in the matter of the ground of the church. We respect Brother Austin-Sparks' spiritual portion, but we disagree with his view concerning the ground of the church. We cannot accept his correction; rather, we would refute his view. This is absolutely a matter of the truth. Those who receive help from Honor Oak have no place to go and no way to advance because they have spirituality without the ground of the church. Therefore, those who leave Honor Oak become wanderers when they go to various places in the world. We cannot allow our brothers to be wandering stars without a definite place. If the churches in Taiwan pursue only spirituality, there will be many problems. Brother Austin-Sparks' emphasis on spirituality is too subjective. He can do this in Honor Oak, but he cannot correct us to match his way. Such a correction will cause our work to fall apart and make us the same as the denominations.

STANDING ON THE LOCAL GROUND AND WALKING ON THE WAY OF THE TRUTH

Even though we might not understand the scope of these matters, my speaking is for our future work in other places. Today there are many believers from different backgrounds. If we want to build the church of the Lord, we need to understand the ground of the church; otherwise, there is no way to have the building. We cannot take the way of exclusion and reject all those from the West. We need to receive them and acknowledge them as brothers. We need proper discernment concerning how to receive those from the West. Otherwise, much of our work will be in vain.

If we think that we should not contend for the ground of locality but should rather be as tolerant as the denominations, then we should save our energy and join them. However, we want God's children to know that God has no way in the denominations, because they cannot produce the building. The best that they can do is lead people to salvation and give them spiritual edification. Over the past thirty years the Lord has shown us that in order to build up the church, we should be spiritual on the one hand and hold on to the ground on the other hand. If we are spiritual but do not have the ground and the building, the brothers will have no way to proceed. If we change our attitude and drop the matter of the ground, the brothers will become wandering stars with no way to proceed.

Every matter has principles and laws. If we do not take the way of the truth, others will, and when those who take the way of the truth question us, we will be speechless. We will not be able to withstand their questioning, because we have not taken the way of the truth. A person may consider that baptism by immersion is unnecessary and that baptism by sprinkling is sufficient. However, when a brother who is baptized by immersion questions him, he will be unable to reply and will fall under the condemnation of the truth. Therefore, for the sake of God's building, we need to have a precise view concerning the ground. Only when we are firm concerning the ground of the church will we have the way to build the church.

We need to love the Lord and be spiritual, and we need to be mingled with God and have His authority so we can be joined together with others. However, we cannot be in the Baptist Church or in the Lutheran Church but only on the ground of locality. On this ground we can speak the truth, and our speaking will be clear and logical. This is the building. The way to build is on the ground. If we do not have the ground, our speaking can only go halfway. We will be the same as Brother Austin-Sparks.

May the Lord have mercy on us that we would clearly see the matter of the ground. We admit that the brothers from the West are good brothers and that their hearts are clean. However, they do not have enough light concerning the truth and therefore are not clear about the ground. They also have a sense of Western superiority that frustrates our ability to help them. If they did not have such a sense and were willing to be humble and fellowship with us concerning the Lord's Word, they would gradually become clear. Their pride causes them to make changes to everything they touch. Hence, they are unable to see the light, and it is difficult for us to help them.

This shows that organized Christianity has problems, and even those who are spiritual and pure have problems. Their conduct and view force us to be passive and maintain a distance even though we do not break off fellowship. However, because there is no active fellowship, it is difficult to have the building. If we were to maintain active fellowship with them, our work would disintegrate. We have a way to advance, but we do not have a way to advance in our relationship with them. Therefore, we would rather maintain our position.

The matter of the church is not simple. We need to see the truth and the ground of the church. We receive all the spiritual riches from those who preceded us over the centuries, regardless of their ground. But we are sure of the way the Lord wants us to take. Nobody can change us in this matter. We admire their spirituality, but this is not our testimony. We know with certainty that the Lord has raised us up for the ground of the church.

When Brother Nee spoke on the principle of the line of

Antioch in 1937, his stress was on the local churches. The notes of the messages were compiled and published as *Rethinking the Work,* now published with the title *The Normal Christian Church Life.* Brother Nee saw this light. Over the past twenty years we have become clearer concerning his speaking. But there is still more to see on this matter. My desire is for us to understand this matter because the administration of the church among us depends on our understanding.

Today transportation in the world is convenient and available to everyone; people come from different places to fellowship with us. The brothers from the West may be spiritual and good, but we must be aware of the problems. I cannot tell you everything, but I beg you to believe me. I am speaking to you earnestly because this is not something I have decided in haste. I have been considering this for several months. I will be held accountable for my words, but you must also understand me correctly. We are not breaking away from the West. We are not an Eastern sect. We need to be clear concerning the Lord's desire when He raised us up. We need to know who we are, what others have, and the help we should receive. Knowing our condition and that of the enemy guarantees victory in every battle. In this way we will not fall short of what the Lord has entrusted to us.

CHAPTER FOURTEEN

THE RECOVERY OF THE CHURCH GROUND

THE BEGINNING OF THE LORD'S RECOVERY

In this chapter we will speak concerning the type of testimony the Lord wants us to bear in this age. Regardless of how much we speak, however, we need a vision and revelation concerning these things so that we may have a genuine seeing.

In the beginning of the work in the East, God gave us the feeling that the condition of Christianity was not proper. Ever since then we have had questions and doubts concerning today's Christianity. These doubts caused us to consider the actual condition of Christianity and to study the Lord's Word. We saw that quite a number of practices in Christianity were not according to the Bible. We abandoned these practices and in each item endeavored to return to the way it was in the beginning according to the Bible. That period could be called the initial stage of the recovery.

In the beginning we did not experience an instantaneous recovery of many items; instead, it was a recovery of item by item. During the first several years many items were recovered. Although items began to be recovered in 1922, we consider that the recovery officially began in 1924. The initial stage of the recovery was completed in 1934.

THE RECOVERY OF THE CHURCH GROUND

When the ground of the church was recovered, the recovery reached the end of the initial stage. By 1925 we were clear that the church should not be divided into sects. The church is one and should be in oneness. It is a sin for the church to be divided into various denominations. We were able to speak a little on the truth concerning sectarianism, but we were not clear concerning the definition of a sect. It was somewhere between 1928 and 1931 that we were able to define sectarianism. We knew that if a church has a particular name, a particular fellowship, and a particular belief, it is a sect. However, we were still not clear concerning the ground of the church.

Even though we were clear that the church is one and should not be divided into sects and we knew the meaning of sectarianism, it was not until 1934 that the light concerning the expression of the church in a locality was clearly and accurately released to all the saints among us. Many of us, however, were clear about the ground of the church in 1932.

BROTHER NEE'S SEEING OF THE CHURCH GROUND

In the first edition of the book *The Orthodoxy of the Church* Brother Nee clearly stated that during a trip to Europe and America in 1933 he came in contact with a number of good Brethren groups. He also contacted a number of reputable spiritual saints and joined their meetings. This was when he first contacted Brother T. Austin-Sparks.

Brother Nee took that trip because he had received an invitation from a Brethren group in London. But he told them that his fellowshipping with them did not mean that he was joining the Brethren assembly. Therefore, he was not restricted by the Brethren when he was in England. He found others, besides the Brethren, who knew the Lord, and he fellowshipped with them. He referred to this in *The Orthodoxy of the Church*. During that trip abroad, Brother Nee visited many places. Some places had the condition of Philadelphia; they showed signs of the revival prophesied by the Lord in the seven epistles in Revelation. Other places were like Laodicea. Since some places had fallen into sin, others maintained a revived condition, and still others had divided repeatedly, it was impossible to make a general statement concerning their condition. After observing the various conditions, particularly the divisions, Brother Nee began to question the basis for the divisions among the Brethren.

He studied and examined all the issues related to the

church in the Bible. After his study, he saw clearly from the Word of God that there is only one church in the universe, but when the church is expressed, it is expressed locality by locality; in other words, there is only one expression of the church in every locality. The repeated divisions among the Brethren caused Brother Nee to study and see the light in God's Word. He saw that the church can have the distinction only of locality. The church in Corinth and the church in Ephesus were two separate churches. The church in Ephesus and the church in Jerusalem were also two separate churches. In addition, in Jerusalem there could not be two or more churches. Similarly, in Ephesus there could not be two or more churches. Brother Nee saw this from God's Word.

Before Brother Nee went overseas in 1933, he was in northern China and stayed in my house for six days. At that time the Lord's work had begun in northern China, but I was still working, so I fellowshipped with him to know what his feeling was concerning whether I should keep my job or serve full time. He only said, "Brother, when you are not clear, you should wait and see." He returned from his trip overseas in the fall. That fall I struggled within because the Lord wanted me to leave my job. At about that time I received a letter from Brother Nee. When he sent the letter, he was aboard a ship in the Mediterranean Sea on his way back from Europe. The letter was a great encouragement and a confirmation to me. It read: "Brother Witness, as for your future, I feel that you should serve the Lord with your full time. How do you feel? May the Lord lead you."

I received the letter more than one month after Brother Nee had written it. By then I had already resigned from my job and had been laboring in Manchuria for three weeks. Upon returning from Manchuria, I read the letter from Brother Nee and was greatly encouraged. The letter was a strong confirmation to me. Even though it had been six months since I parted with Brother Nee and he did not usually correspond with me, he sent such a simple, clear, timely word concerning leaving my job and serving full time. The most amazing thing was that Brother Nee wrote the letter at about the same time I was struggling before the Lord whether to leave my job.

I felt deeply that this was the Lord's leading in this matter, so I determined to go to Shanghai to see Brother Nee. In the fall I went to Shanghai. That was my first visit to Shanghai.

It was about that time that Brother Nee said he clearly saw the light concerning the ground of locality. He had just returned from England, and he saw this matter in the Word of God. On the spiritual side, it was also at this time that he saw the central light concerning Christ as God's centrality and universality. Therefore, he decided to call a national conference in January 1934. While I was in Shanghai, Brother Nee asked me to assist him in replying to some letters concerning spiritual matters. I wrote a long letter on behalf of Brother Nee to Brother Hsieh Tien En from Canton. This letter was later published in *Collection of Newsletters* (see *The Collected Works of Watchman Nee,* vol. 25, pp. 77-80, 107-117). The letter was mainly regarding denominations. At that time we paid much attention to spiritual matters and denominations. Only Brother Nee was clear regarding the ground; the rest of us had not seen it. We knew only that the church should be one and that denominations were wrong.

THE CONFIRMATION OF THE CHURCH GROUND

The letter I wrote to Brother Hsieh Tien En was my first article published by Brother Nee's Gospel Book Room. I labored very much in writing this article, and although it was a letter, it was like a booklet in content. Many points in the letter were concerning denominations; it defined a denomination and the meaning of denominationalism. At the time I personally was not clear regarding the ground of the church. I knew what oneness was and what a denomination was, and I could speak concerning them. However, I did not know the ground of the church. The other co-workers were also unclear. Only Brother Nee was clear.

About one hundred twenty brothers and sisters from northern China attended the conference in January. This special gathering was a turning point for the advance of the church. It also influenced me personally. From the fellowship we saw the sin of sectarianism and the need for the oneness of the

THE RECOVERY OF THE CHURCH GROUND 179

church. Therefore, some co-workers were burdened concerning this matter and determined to take this way.

After the conference, I returned by boat to northern China. Many brothers who attended the conference remained in Shanghai and requested that Brother Nee hold Bible-study meetings to help them know how to meet. This was because meetings were being raised up with ones who left the denominations and the sects, but they did not know how to meet. Brother Nee agreed, and the manuscripts were later edited and published as the book *The Assembly Life.*

I was not present during these meetings, having already returned to northern China. When I returned to Shanghai four months later, I heard about the Bible study but did not see any notes. It was only after Brother Nee finished editing the manuscript, that he gave it to me and asked me to write a preface. I carefully read the messages and understood the content of the entire Bible study. Since then I have been deeply impressed that the expression of the church is local. The word *expression,* however, was not used then. We began to use the word *expression* in 1950 in Taiwan when we defined the boundary of a local church. It was also about that time in 1934 that we began to fellowship concerning the matter of locality, and the light concerning locality was confirmed. When the light concerning locality was confirmed, the ground of the church was also confirmed among us.

During the January conference Brother Nee released clear messages on Christ as God's centrality, and he became very clear concerning the ground of the church. As a result, 1934 was a milestone in the Lord's recovery, and we entered into another stage. We saw that Christ as God's centrality and universality is the content of the church and that outwardly the church should take the ground of locality. After this, Brother Nee was not the only one who was clear concerning all these matters; we, his co-workers, were also clear.

BELIEVERS ENTHUSIASTICALLY LEAVING
THE DENOMINATIONS

By 1934 a number of people were leaving the denominations. It was becoming a trend, and almost everywhere there was an enthusiastic response. Every day we received many letters and most of them were concerning leaving the denominations. All the letters were given to me because I was the acting editor of *Collection of Newsletters*. From these letters we learned of many stories of ones who left the denominations. We received letters from the northern, southern, and central parts of China. Leaving the denominations even caused problems among the Western missionaries. Some of the missionaries from the China Inland Mission called a special meeting to discuss how to deal with the situation. In the eyes of Christianity, it was a revolution. Everywhere many were leaving the denominations.

Those who left the denominations followed a general practice to leave openly, not secretly. In most cases, they would write and sign an official letter requesting their denomination to remove their names from the membership registry. It was done rather officially. Although this was not a regulation, the general practice was to write an official letter declaring one's decision to leave the denomination. Believers were leaving with intense fervor and vigor.

THE TESTIMONY TO BE MAINTAINED

At the beginning of 1935 a few co-workers felt that the trend of leaving the denominations was not correct, because it involved many complicated issues. Therefore, Brother Nee spoke to the co-workers to clarify the matter of our testimony. He said that leaving the denominations is not our testimony; rather, our testimony is Christ: Christ as the Savior, Christ as life, Christ as the conquering King, Christ as the Lord of all things, Christ as God's centrality, and Christ as God's universality. He also pointed out that the testimony of Christ is absolutely in the church and that the church is one and the ground of the church is local. All these matters were made very clear. In 1937 Brother Nee spoke further on how to maintain the Lord's testimony by establishing churches locality by locality. These messages were collected and published in *Rethinking the Work,* now published with the title *The Normal Christian Church Life.*

The Lord raised us up in the East to maintain the testimony

of Christ being expressed in the church. Such a testimony includes saving people and making them spiritual. It also includes the building up of the saints, locality by locality, to be a corporate dwelling place of God and the Body of Christ so that Christ can be expressed through this corporate vessel. Although the church is expressed in different localities, all the local churches should be one in testimony and have fellowship with one another. This is what the Lord showed us, and this is the testimony He wants us to maintain.

THE LORD'S SPECIAL COMMISSION TO US

We acknowledge that God has used different ways and many workers to save thousands of people. Not so much with us as with others, God has done much related to salvation. In fact, we need to learn from others concerning the many ways to lead people to salvation. God has also done much related to life through others, and their work was quite good. This is true in the Western world and also in China. The Lord has done much in the East and in the West related to helping people to be spiritual, to consecrate themselves, to love Him, to live before Him, to fear Him, and to walk with Him.

However, the Lord has given us a special commission related to one church in one locality, the building, and the expression of the Body. Besides us, no one else has paid attention to these matters. We are the only ones who have paid attention to these matters, and we are even opposed because of this. We have been attacked by many outsiders mainly because of these points. They say that it is sufficient to save others and help them to be spiritual but that there is no need to be concerned about meeting and being built up in every locality to be the expression of Christ's Body. They argue that if we would simply be concerned about salvation and spirituality, there would be no problems concerning denominations, the church, and the ground of the church. They argue that people could be saved in the Catholic Church and in the Presbyterian Church and that they could also be spiritual in the Catholic Church and in the Presbyterian Church.

Some believers feel that they could be spiritual on their own; they also feel that since they were spiritual, they could be united to be one in the spirit. Some of those who have felt this way have included Mr. Chia, the top pastor in the Presbyterian Church, Mr. Kao, the top pastor in the Quaker Church, and Mr. Cheng, a spiritual Christian worker. They were all very spiritual. They thought that since they were in Christ and in the Holy Spirit, they could be united to form a spiritual group that would take care of the work together. So they published a magazine called *The Spiritual Light* and invited Sister Ruth Lee to be the editor. In 1925, after seeing the oneness of the church and the sin of denominationalism, Sister Ruth Lee was no longer willing to serve as the editor and decided to resign. The pastors, however, did not agree. Later when the Chinese Nationalist government was engaged in a fight against the warlords, some Communist soldiers in the Nationalist army burned the church buildings in Nanking and arrested the preachers. The office of *The Spiritual Light* was not spared.

I respected these spiritual people. I can still testify with a pure conscience that they were devout Christians who lived in the Lord's presence. However, the ground of locality and the building up of the Body of Christ are not simply matters that we minister; they are related to our testimony. I have spoken with both Pastor Chia and Pastor Cheng. I could only humbly receive their spiritual instruction, confessing that they were God-fearing, spiritual, senior brothers who lived in the presence of God. However, they neither knew nor understood that God has commissioned us with the testimony of the local expression of the Body. They even exhorted me not to insist on this point.

Once in 1937 I happened to be on the same train with Pastor Cheng. Though I cannot remember the details of our conversation, I do remember that he exhorted me not to be so insistent. He said that it is good enough for us to preach the gospel diligently to save souls and to speak the truth of God for others to be nurtured and perfected. He said that this is the highest point of a Christian. His attitude was sincere, and he truly treasured and admired us. From our manner of speaking and our attitude, he knew that we were clear concerning the truth and had a firm foundation. Therefore, Pastor Cheng and even Pastor Chia treasured us. We also respected them greatly before the Lord as we would respect our seniors. We also had fellowship with a Pastor Ting, and we respected him. Pastor Ting was in his seventies when I was in my thirties. He was an elderly person living in the Lord's presence. We respected him and loved him, and he also loved and treasured us.

These elderly brothers felt that it was precious that young people like us were willing to forsake our future and live for the Lord. They highly regarded us. However, they always felt that we were too much. They once indicated that we were the top group among the Chinese Christians and that if we would change and take the middle road, we would become the center of the churches in China, and the future of the churches in China would depend on us. According to their view, we were extreme in our attitude.

However, we saw that the Lord's testimony is dispensational. These elderly believers saw something in their generation, but it was not the Lord's intention for us to keep the testimony of their generation. The Lord is moving, and He desires to advance. For this reason, although we respected their portion, we knew that God desired to take another step in China. The Lord desires more than personal salvation and spirituality; He desires to work out the testimony of His Body, the testimony of the church, in locality after locality so that He can gain a corporate vessel for His expression. This is what the Lord showed us more than twenty years ago.

Over the past twenty years, we have had many experiences and have suffered many blows. Even though we were somewhat affected by them, we have not given up the testimony entrusted to us. There have been spiritual persons and evangelical giants who have influenced us. We were inferior to them in the power of the gospel and also concerning certain spiritual matters. Nevertheless, we felt that we had a testimony to maintain. Sometimes we wondered whether we were extreme. We wondered why those who had power in the gospel and those who were spiritual would not pay attention to the testimony of the church. We were often tested in this matter. However, we can testify that we became clearer every time we were tested. Today the Lord's intention on earth is not merely to gain souls or spiritual persons; rather, His desire is to build up His corporate testimony in every locality. We are very clear concerning this.

PROBLEMS WE ENCOUNTERED AND OUR SOLUTION

We studied how to deal with the difficulties brought to us by those who were powerful in the gospel and were spiritual but who did not bear this testimony. We sought the Lord, asking what type of attitude we should have toward them. Indeed, there were some who were powerful in the gospel. For example, Dr. John Sung was an evangelist when we became clear concerning this testimony in 1935. He went everywhere preaching the gospel. Whether his jumping, kicking, shouting, and weeping were in the flesh or had an element of the Spirit, wherever he went, thousands of people repented when he preached. He was powerful in the gospel, but he always rebuked us. We did not know what attitude we should have toward him, and the co-workers among us considered this to be a serious problem.

There was also Pastor Chia, who was weighty in the truth and held a high position among theologians. Although he treasured us, he opposed us for taking this way. A distinguished theological school, the Chinese Women's Seminary in River Bay, Shanghai, also opposed us and forbade its students from attending our meetings in Shanghai. It was difficult for us to know what our attitude should be when we were opposed by those who were powerful in the gospel or had spiritual weight.

In the spring of 1934 Brother Nee and I went to River Bay by car. It was a long journey during which he expressed his feelings in our conversation. He asked me what I felt we should do since so many were against us. We could not deny that some preached the gospel with much power. We also could not deny that others were truly spiritual; they led others to love the Lord, spoke concerning the way of the cross, and edified others in the truth. However, they rejected us. We were tested in this matter and did not know what attitude we should have.

After much consideration, study, fellowship, and seeking of

the Lord, eventually all the co-workers felt that we could not give up our testimony, and we could not leave the ground on which we stood. We could accept the gospel preached in power, and we could accept the spiritual matters, including the perfecting in truth and life, but we absolutely could not waver concerning the ground and the testimony. We could fellowship with other believers on spiritual matters, receiving and sharing spiritual things with them. We should fellowship mutually in the gospel, in spiritual matters, and in the truth, but we could not compromise the church ground. We decided that this should be our attitude.

We tried to receive spiritual things from others; we accepted things related to the gospel and the truth. However, this attitude gave Brother Yu Cheng-hwa the boldness to accept all the things of Madame Guyon, including some things of Catholicism. He did this because the co-workers had adopted an attitude of receiving anything related to the gospel, spirituality, or the truth that a person had, regardless of their denomination or sect, without sacrificing our ground.

In the co-workers' meeting held in Shanghai in 1937, we fellowshipped concerning the line of Antioch. Brother Nee then suggested that we proceed in two ways. On one hand, we would all go to different places and establish meetings in order to propagate; on the other hand, those of us who were clear concerning the truth would try to labor in the denominations, releasing the truth and giving them a spiritual supply. After this fellowship we began to carry out the work in these aspects.

Shortly after that fellowship, however, the war with Japan began. This caused the propagation work to stop. At that time, there were many intellectuals among us; many brothers and sisters were working in the medical or educational fields. During the war, many of them moved to provinces that were farther from the war front, and they evacuated from places that were occupied by the Japanese, such as Nanking. It was not until the end of the war that we again began to meet in these places. During the war, Satan was working and dealt Brother Nee a heavy blow. As a result, those who moved away from the war did not receive much supply, and the believers in territories occupied by the enemy were weak. Thus, the testimony was weakened in all the places.

In this weakened condition we saw that those in the denominations were more effective in the gospel, they were the same as us in spirituality, and they had produced ones who understood the truth. It seemed as if leaving the denominations was our only accomplishment. Our situation was gloomy and dismal. After the war the leading ones experienced great difficulties with one another because they had gone through a long period of being neglected, tried, and frustrated. The churches suffered various trials. When the saints returned to Shanghai, all the co-workers gathered together and fellowshipped. Based on our feeling and our past experiences, we decided that we must keep the testimony that we saw in the beginning, the testimony of one local church in one locality and that we must build all spiritual things on this ground. We would accept things of the gospel, spirituality, and the truth from other denominations or sects. The only thing we would not relinquish and would insist upon was the ground of the church. We would insist on taking the ground of one locality for one church; we would hold on to the testimony of the Body of Christ.

A WORD OF FELLOWSHIP
CONCERNING BROTHER T. AUSTIN-SPARKS

Our relationship with Brother Austin-Sparks was not based on the ground of the church; rather, it was based on spiritual matters. We were clear concerning the Lord's desire for us in the East; we also felt that we should receive a supply from other ministries. Even though other ministries might not have a clear ground, position, or background, they do have a portion in the spiritual ministry. This principle applies to those who are alive and to those who have passed away. Madame Guyon, for instance, had a spiritual ministry, but she was a Catholic. The fact that she was in Catholicism should not be a reason for us to reject the spiritual supply from her portion. However, this does not mean that we will receive the things of Catholicism. According to this principle, we should receive the supply from Dr. F. B. Meyer, Andrew

Murray, and Mrs. Jessie Penn-Lewis. We received all the spiritual riches that we could find in the books written over the centuries, whether they were related to the gospel, life, or truth. However, we rejected their stand, that is, the organization they represented, because it did not correspond with our testimony and would even damage our testimony.

Brother Nee fellowshipped with Brother Austin-Sparks concerning this matter. Brother Nee also did his best to receive the spiritual help from Brother Austin-Sparks' group, but the ground of the church was not a factor in our relationship with Brother Austin-Sparks. For this reason, Brother Nee said that Brother Austin-Sparks was not as clear as we were related to the ground of the church, and we did not ask Brother Austin-Sparks his position concerning the ground.

OUR ATTITUDE TOWARD BROTHER AUSTIN-SPARKS

Brother Austin-Sparks' group in London has left the denominations. Hence, he is clearer in his standing than Andrew Murray and more advanced than Dr. Meyer or Mrs. Penn-Lewis. Therefore, on the positive side, he is nearly irreproachable. On the negative side, however, he is not as definite as we who are in the East. We saw that the ground of the church is unique and that there should be only one church in one locality. We were very clear concerning this point from the beginning. Even though we differ from Brother Austin-Sparks regarding the ground, this did not cause us to reject him or his spiritual supply. Our attitude was to receive the spiritual supply from all the ministries the Lord has given to His church over the centuries, regardless of their standing or background. We would not be affected by their background. This was our attitude.

Since Brother Austin-Sparks' view differs from ours related to the ground, Brother Nee said that the time had not yet come to invite him. Not only so, Brother Austin-Sparks also has a certain spiritual influence on others; hence, if we had invited him to China, it would have caused a problem. It was not until later that we understood this. I am mentioning this so that we can see our testimony and the proper attitude we should maintain regarding this testimony.

PROBLEMS BROUGHT IN THROUGH BROTHER AUSTIN-SPARKS' SECOND VISIT TO TAIWAN

Brother Austin-Sparks' first visit to Taiwan was for our spiritual supply. It did not cause any problems because we did not touch the ground. It was a very pleasant time. His second visit, however, caused us much grief. Brother Austin-Sparks should have maintained the attitude of ministering a spiritual supply and should not have touched the ground. If he had done this, there would not have been any problems. However, in his second trip Brother Austin-Sparks overstepped the boundary of his ministry and not only inquired concerning the practice of the church ground but also interfered.

A brother suggested that perhaps I misunderstood Brother Austin-Sparks. I had also hoped that it was a misunderstanding and that Brother Austin-Sparks did not oppose us on this matter. During his visit a number of saints began to waver, considering that it was not necessary to pay attention to the ground but that it was sufficient to be spiritual. This proves that it was not a misunderstanding.

Brother Austin-Sparks reprimanded us openly, not just in private conversations. In a meeting he openly said, "You limit Christ to a locality and thus make Christ a small Christ and the church a small church." This word proves that he insisted on his view. This was the problem we encountered.

We should be clear concerning the testimony the Lord desires us to keep in His recovery. We thank the Lord for anyone among us who is powerful in the gospel for the salvation of souls. However, we will be troubled if you act or speak in a way that affects the ground and our testimony. As long as what you do does not affect this testimony and the ground, you can exercise your portion, and we will welcome you and regard you as a co-worker, a dear brother or sister. We are not narrow.

For example, there was a sister in Hong Kong who did not see the ground but had spiritual fellowship with us. This sister had a burden to serve the Lord in the East. Because she wanted to be with a group of God's children whom she considered to be pleasing to God's will and who were spiritual, she chose us. Her joining us was related to the spiritual supply, not the ground. We, therefore, received her as our co-worker even though she was not clear concerning the ground. This is because, spiritually speaking, she truly was our co-worker. She did not interfere with our practice concerning the ground. She endeavored to exercise her portion so that the brothers and sisters could be edified. We recognized her supply, and we did not compel her to be one with us concerning the ground. She did not have problems with us. However, she needed to be clear that she joined a group of brothers and sisters who were standing on the ground. They were united on the ground. Even if the leading ones among them turned away to love the world, they would still take this way, because this is the way the Lord desires.

THERE BEING NO RECONCILIATION OUTSIDE THE GROUND

Since we have seen the ground, we must keep it steadfastly. There is no room for a middle ground. There is no neutral ground. If the ground of denomination is right, we should not have another ground; we should all worship God in the denominations. If the ground of denomination is wrong, there can be no reconciliation with it. We need to be absolutely clear concerning this point.

Reconciliation will not issue in blessing. On the contrary, it causes both sides to suffer. There have been many cases of compromise among us. Some cases involved individuals, and others involved a group; some took place in southern China and others, in northern China. The result was always damage and loss; neither side was edified, and all our labor turned out to be in vain. Furthermore, most of the ones who attempted to reconcile with the denominations eventually went the way of the denominations. Consequently, they became people without a vision. We should never think that those in the denominations can help us. We must realize that not only can they not help us, but also if we reconcile with them, they will influence us.

In northern China I was jailed and tortured by the Japanese because I was not willing to compromise. If I had compromised with the denominations, I would not have been jailed, and there would not have been so many problems. I was put into prison because I was unwilling to cooperate with the denominations. Our friends in the denominations wanted to pull me to their side, to make me the same as they, but I stood firm. Hence, they spoke unfavorably about me to the Japanese military police, who eventually put me in prison. After three weeks of interrogation, the Japanese military police could not find any evidence against me. They said, "Mr. Lee, we have interrogated you for three and a half weeks, but we cannot find anything wrong with you...Why is it that those in Christianity do not speak well of you?" Their question made me realize that those in the denominations had spoken all kinds of evil words concerning me to the Japanese.

The president of the United Christian Association, who was a classmate and neighbor of a brother among us, heard about my arrest by the Japanese. Before I was imprisoned, a pastor's wife spoke to a crowd in front of her house, expressing her joy that the Japanese were about to discipline me. Since I never cooperated with the denominations, they wanted the Japanese to discipline me. I was truly under the threat of death when I was in prison, because it was as easy for the Japanese military police to kill a Chinese as it was to kill a chicken. The Lord kept my life during that time.

After I was freed from prison, our friends in the denominations again asked me to cooperate with them. They did not compel me; instead, I was informed that twelve congregations would participate in a conference and that a speaker from each congregation would deliver a sermon. They also told me on which day I should give a sermon. I told the brothers that even if I should die, I would not give that sermon. Then an elderly brother accompanied me to visit the president of the United Christian Association, because I felt that, by courtesy, I should let him know that I could not accept the assignment.

The president of the United Christian Association felt that I should consider the matter and pray about it. When I said that there was no need to pray, he said, "Mr. Lee, what you are doing is very dangerous." I solemnly replied, "Since you have said this, I would like to tell you that the most you can do is to have me arrested and put in prison again." It was difficult to believe that they used the expression *dangerous* when asking for my cooperation. I believe that this was the enemy's scheme to force us to be the same as Christianity. At the time those in Christianity detested our being different from them. If we would reconcile with them and be the same as they were, the enemy would applaud loudly because his scheme had succeeded.

What God has shown us is not merely a matter of salvation or of spirituality. He has shown us where a Christian should and should not be. This is the testimony we have borne for over thirty years. Satan, however, has been pulling us away from this testimony, wanting us to reconcile with Christianity. When this happens, Satan has succeeded. Therefore, we should be clear and see our need to maintain this difference.

THE PRACTICE OF THE GROUND BRINGING IN THE BLESSING

Brother Austin-Sparks did not know this when he came to Taiwan. He left Taiwan in March and arrived in London in April. In May he wrote an article for his magazine in which he praised us, saying, "For many days I spoke to more than five hundred select Christian workers during the day and to about two thousand believers at night. Furthermore, we visited churches for several days, and everyone we met was zealous. Their faces were shining, waiting to fellowship with us. They devoured every word we spoke." He gave us a top compliment.

However, I would like to ask Brother Austin-Sparks if he knows the main reason for the success of our work. Perhaps many would think that the main reason is the work of the Holy Spirit. We agree. However, why would the Holy Spirit not bless the work on other grounds? I believe that Brother Austin-Sparks met many Western missionaries and people from other groups when he was in Taiwan. They all labored zealously. They have more resources than we have and are more talented than we are. Some among them are even better educated than we are and have higher reputations. Why did Brother Austin-Sparks not praise their work? Why does the Holy Spirit not do a work among them?

We are clear that if we have any result that is worthy of praise, it is because we have not reconciled with the denominations. If from 1949 we had worked in reconciliation with the denominations, we would not have had the same result. The main reason that our work can be praised is that we have the ground. Regrettably, Brother Austin-Sparks saw the result, but he did not see the reason for the result.

THE GROUND OF LOCALITY BEING THE BASIS FOR OUR EXISTENCE

I realize that Brother Austin-Sparks adjusted us because of his care for us. He did not have bad intentions. However, he was like a doctor who gave the wrong diagnosis; what he perceived as a sickness is actually our very life. The local ground is not a sickness. If this item is removed, we cannot live any longer.

This can be compared to a person who drinks tea and then breaks the teapot. He does not realize that the teapot is needed to brew more tea. The tea depends on the teapot for its existence. The blessing we experience is because we stand on the ground of locality. We depend on the ground for our existence; we are being upheld by the ground. Therefore, if we allow others to take away our ground, our "teapot," not only will the teapot they hate disappear, but the tea they love will also vanish.

Thus, it is not a matter of whether one has a good or a bad intention; we never doubted Brother Austin-Sparks' intention. He cared for us out of a pure and fervent heart. We treasured this. However, the ground is a matter of light, not of a personal view. This fellowship is so that we may be clear. If we ignore this fellowship, history will be repeated, and there will not be a blessing.

RECEIVING OTHERS WITHOUT DAMAGING THE LORD'S TESTIMONY

Over the past two thousand years God has raised up many useful ministries. In America there are ministries that are strong in the gospel. God is great, and He has raised up many spiritual persons. Brother Austin-Sparks is an example.

Although Brother Austin-Sparks stands on a ground that is close to the local ground, he is not on the local ground. There have been many who have had such a stand in history. Some, who do not stand on the local ground, have received more revelation from the Bible than we have. We are happy to receive the supply from them because these are the riches that God has given to His church. Even some who were in Catholicism, such as Madame Guyon and Brother Lawrence, were people with much spiritual weight and gifts. We should receive the spiritual supply from all of them.

At the same time, however, we should be very clear that the Lord raised us up for the testimony of the one Body so that there will be an expression of a built-up representation in each locality. We are not demanding that all the brothers and sisters have this vision. However, we would ask all the co-workers, whether brothers or sisters, to try their best to minister in the gospel and in the truth and not to touch or destroy the ground of the church. If they are willing to cooperate, there will be no problems; however, if they touch or destroy the ground, they will cause much trouble.

May the Lord grant us grace to become clearer concerning these messages as we go on. We should be clear concerning where we are, and we should be humble to receive what can benefit us in the gospel, the truth, and the spiritual supply. However, we must be absolutely clear related to the testimony the Lord wants us to bear. We should guard this testimony securely. We should not be foolish—guarding the vision yet not standing on the ground; neither should we guard the ground and reject the spiritual riches.

If we are clear concerning this point, we will be able to help those who come in contact with us. We receive the spiritual supply from others, and we also render them the help. We should receive help from others in humility, and we should also know our testimony and our ground. We should always render some help to others when we contact them. We should not speak of things that will not edify them. This is to do all things for the building up. We should not shrink from speaking whatever is beneficial to them. If we can help others in this way without forsaking our stand, the Lord's testimony will be built up.

We should receive Brother Austin-Sparks' portion. The problem was that Brother Austin-Sparks overstepped his portion and damaged us. Moreover, the problem was enlarged because some of our brothers were not clear. If Brother Austin-Sparks had not overstepped his portion, there would not have been problems. Likewise, if our brothers were all clear, there would not have been problems even though Brother Austin-Sparks had overstepped. Therefore, the key is for us to be clear concerning the ground. If we are clear, no one can easily sway us. People can say whatever they desire, and we will not waver.

We still have a normal relationship with Brother Austin-Sparks; it has not been damaged. What we are stressing is that it is difficult for us to accept what differs from us in the matter of the ground and in the matter of the light of this truth, because the ground is our very life, and it affects our testimony.

AVOIDING AN ATTITUDE OF SUPERIORITY IN THE WORK

It is a problem that the brothers from the West have an attitude of superiority. However, we should not oppose them because of this, nor should we react negatively or look down on them. The only serious problem is our differing view concerning the ground. Their superior attitude hindered further fellowship. Even though this was unintentional, it was revealed unconsciously in their behavior.

Let me illustrate. Because I am from northern China, I unconsciously speak with a northern accent. I do not intend to speak with a northern accent, but as I speak, the accent comes out. I was born and raised in northern China, I also lived there for many years. I am composed of the elements of northern China. Unless I am transformed, my northern accent will always be with me. As long as I live, I will unconsciously have a Chinese flavor and a northern Chinese accent. Similarly, the various influences of international politics over the past one hundred years and China's position in international politics has caused the brothers from the West to have an attitude of superiority that is difficult to remove. In addition, our history over the past decades has caused us to have an attitude of inferiority.

This is a problem in the East and in the West. I have been praying concerning this matter for a long time. May the Lord cover me with His blood; I would now like to fight against this matter, endeavoring to get rid of these attitudes of inferiority in the East and superiority in the West. May these attitudes no longer exist in the future when the brothers and sisters from the East and from the West come together to fellowship. Presently it is not a problem for the believers in the East to receive the spiritual help from those in the West. We are already doing it. However, the believers in the West will need to be humble in order to receive spiritual supply from the believers in the East. When there is this open fellowship, the Lord will reveal what we have seen to the believers in the West. I strongly believe that soon the brothers from the West will come and live in the East for a period of time in order to learn. They will then understand what the Lord is doing on this earth today. They will understand the way the Lord is taking today. Only time can prove this word.

Many of you brothers are in your twenties. If the Lord delays His return, you will probably live longer on this earth than I will. One day perhaps you will recall this word. This is the Lord's mercy to us, and we should not be proud. We should be clear concerning what the Lord has given to the church over the past two thousand years, and we should understand the significance of the Lord's raising us up in the East in this age. May we be faithful to learn our lessons and labor in the Lord's work, and may we refrain from comparing ourselves with others. As long as we are faithful, the result is up to the Lord, not up to us.

About the Author

Witness Lee was born in 1905 in northern China and raised in a Christian family. At age 19 he was fully captured for Christ and immediately consecrated himself to preach the gospel for the rest of his life. Early in his service, he met Watchman Nee, a renowned preacher, teacher, and writer. Witness Lee labored together with Watchman Nee under his direction. In 1934 Watchman Nee entrusted Witness Lee with the responsibility for his publication operation, called the Shanghai Gospel Bookroom.

Prior to the Communist takeover in 1949, Witness Lee was sent by Watchman Nee and his other co-workers to Taiwan to ensure that the things delivered to them by the Lord would not be lost. Watchman Nee instructed Witness Lee to continue the former's publishing operation abroad as the Taiwan Gospel Bookroom, which has been publicly recognized as the publisher of Watchman Nee's works outside China. Witness Lee's work in Taiwan manifested the Lord's abundant blessing. From a mere 350 believers, newly fled from the mainland, the churches in Taiwan grew to 20,000 in five years.

In 1962 Witness Lee felt led of the Lord to come to the United States, settling in California. During his 35 years of service in the U.S., he ministered in weekly meetings and weekend conferences, delivering several thousand spoken messages. Much of his speaking has since been published as over 400 titles. Many of these have been translated into over fourteen languages. He gave his last public conference in February 1997 at the age of 91.

He leaves behind a prolific presentation of the truth in the Bible. His major work, *Life-study of the Bible,* comprises over 25,000 pages of commentary on every book of the Bible from the perspective of the believers' enjoyment and experience of God's divine life in Christ through the Holy Spirit. Witness Lee was the chief editor of a new translation of the New Testament into Chinese called the Recovery Version and directed the translation of the same into English. The Recovery Version also appears in a number of other languages. He provided an extensive body of footnotes, outlines, and spiritual cross references. A radio broadcast of his messages can be heard on Christian radio stations in the United States. In 1965 Witness Lee founded Living Stream Ministry, a non-profit corporation, located in Anaheim, California, which officially presents his and Watchman Nee's ministry.

Witness Lee's ministry emphasizes the experience of Christ as life and the practical oneness of the believers as the Body of Christ. Stressing the importance of attending to both these matters, he led the churches under his care to grow in Christian life and function. He was unbending in his conviction that God's goal is not narrow sectarianism but the Body of Christ. In time, believers began to meet simply as the church in their localities in response to this conviction. In recent years a number of new churches have been raised up in Russia and in many eastern European countries.

OTHER BOOKS PUBLISHED BY
Living Stream Ministry

Titles by Witness Lee:

Abraham—Called by God	0-7363-0359-6
The Experience of Life	0-87083-417-7
The Knowledge of Life	0-87083-419-3
The Tree of Life	0-87083-300-6
The Economy of God	0-87083-415-0
The Divine Economy	0-87083-268-9
God's New Testament Economy	0-87083-199-2
The World Situation and God's Move	0-87083-092-9
Christ vs. Religion	0-87083-010-4
The All-inclusive Christ	0-87083-020-1
Gospel Outlines	0-87083-039-2
Character	0-87083-322-7
The Secret of Experiencing Christ	0-87083-227-1
The Life and Way for the Practice of the Church Life	0-87083-785-0
The Basic Revelation in the Holy Scriptures	0-87083-105-4
The Crucial Revelation of Life in the Scriptures	0-87083-372-3
The Spirit with Our Spirit	0-87083-798-2
Christ as the Reality	0-87083-047-3
The Central Line of the Divine Revelation	0-87083-960-8
The Full Knowledge of the Word of God	0-87083-289-1
Watchman Nee—A Seer of the Divine Revelation ...	0-87083-625-0

Titles by Watchman Nee:

How to Study the Bible	0-7363-0407-X
God's Overcomers	0-7363-0433-9
The New Covenant	0-7363-0088-0
The Spiritual Man 3 volumes	0-7363-0269-7
Authority and Submission	0-7363-0185-2
The Overcoming Life	1-57593-817-0
The Glorious Church	0-87083-745-1
The Prayer Ministry of the Church	0-87083-860-1
The Breaking of the Outer Man and the Release ...	1-57593-955-X
The Mystery of Christ	1-57593-954-1
The God of Abraham, Isaac, and Jacob	0-87083-932-2
The Song of Songs	0-87083-872-5
The Gospel of God 2 volumes	1-57593-953-3
The Normal Christian Church Life	0-87083-027-9
The Character of the Lord's Worker	1-57593-322-5
The Normal Christian Faith	0-87083-748-6
Watchman Nee's Testimony	0-87083-051-1

Available at
Christian bookstores, or contact Living Stream Ministry
2431 W. La Palma Ave. • Anaheim, CA 92801
1-800-549-5164 • www.livingstream.com